Build It Yourself

Build It Yourself

Weekend Projects for the Garden

Frank Perrone

Photographs by Nicholas Perrone
Illustrations by Christopher Perrone

Princeton Architectural Press
New York

This book is dedicated to my family:
To my wife, Linda, thank you for your constant support through the peaks and valleys of life. Without your guidance and strength, none of this would have been possible.
My sons, Christopher and Nicholas, were equal partners on this project. I couldn't have done this without your help.
You guys are golden!

Contents

7.

8.

9.

10.

11.

12.

Introduction

"Take a pencil, draw something on the wood, and cut it out"—these were my only instructions. My cousin Marie, who watched my brother and I during our summer breaks, had run out of interesting things for us to do and offered to take us to PS 83 in the Bronx for an activity. The room, PS 83's cafeteria, was packed with kids, and it smelled of freshly cut pine. A tall boy took me by the arm and literally swung me into a chair. He grabbed a piece of wood and then handed me a saw. His instructions were brief and to the point. As I turned back to ask for help, he looked me square in the eye and said, "Build it yourself." At first I was totally confused, but then I realized the only option was to watch what everyone else was doing and then cut. That's how it all began…

A big part of that summer was my close relationship with my grandfather Francesco. I followed him everywhere he went, and we usually wound up at his workshop or in his vegetable garden. His workshop was filled to the rafters with all types of hand tools, gardening supplies, and a lot of miscellaneous items. Since he had gotten older, his garden, which had been about three acres, had shrunk to a third of its original size. My grandfather's vegetable garden was the place that united our family. Those gatherings turned into social events that lasted into the night. It was exciting to see everyone come together to harvest the vegetables and to squeeze the grapes into wine. We spent a lot of hot days hammering leftover pieces of wood together to support his grapevine. His real pride and joy, though, was his fig tree. It stood two stories high, and to harvest its fruit, he had to build a scaffold around it. When we worked together, my grandfather would encourage me to take my time. Patience and persistence were the two greatest lessons he taught me. I can't remember a day we weren't building or growing something. I learned so much of my craft by watching him. He would use whatever he had on hand to build a project, and most projects were developed as we went along. I rarely saw him use a ruler. As a project started to take shape, he would take a step back, tilt his head, take a quick glance, and say we needed to do more. Repurposing old projects into new ones was something we did every day. It was second nature to him. What I learned best from him was to build with whatever wood or tools you have on hand and to trust your instincts.

I also got a lot from the well-thought-out and organized format of the master carpenter Norm Abrams's PBS series *The New Yankee Workshop.* I would videotape the show so that I could play it back and study all of the tools and techniques from each episode. The early years of that show shaped how and what I build today.

As my professional career began to progress, I was challenged with all types of projects, and as they became more complex, I needed a better source of information. The internet was in its infancy, and the best resources were either the public libraries or bookstores. So I compiled a collection of books and magazines that included a variety of styles and techniques. I would learn the techniques needed for a project, compile the information, and then teach it to my staff. As my company and staff grew, I began developing a teaching and learning environment. When hiring staff, I always tried to find people that had no previous woodworking experience but a strong desire to learn.

As my career took twists and turns, I found a home at Wave Hill, a public garden and cultural center in the Bronx. This is where I established a series of novice woodworking classes. All of the projects and techniques were created for beginners, with no experience required.

A friend of mine once asked me, "What is so exciting about introducing novices to woodworking?" I see novice woodworkers as blank canvases ready to be painted. They haven't yet learned any bad woodworking habits. When something does go wrong, I don't jump in to fix their project for them. Instead, I challenge them by asking the question: "Why do you think this happened?" This helps them take ownership of their project and they gain confidence in their ability. To ease any early apprehension, I tell stories about how I started in woodworking or the funny mistakes I've made; they reciprocate with fond memories about a piece of furniture their great-uncle or grandfather made and how much they cherish it. Sometimes they will even confess to me about a failed project, or ask my advice about how to repair something. At each class, we become so engrossed in what we're doing that we block out what's going on outside the room. As they move closer to completing their project and start to see it take shape, finishing becomes the high point of every class. As we wrap up each class, congratulations are shared with everyone, telephone numbers are exchanged, photos are taken, and Facebook pages are updated. Seeing my students beam with pride while standing next to their projects, always looking forward to my next class is the reason I teach woodworking to novices. For me, it doesn't get any better than that!

McCloskey
Spar Varnish
SPAX

Getting Started

This book is a collection of projects and techniques created for beginners. A good starting point for any novice woodworker is to make sure to familiarize yourself with the tools you intend to use. Each project can be built using basic woodworking tools. In this section, I will go over the general rules and tools used for any woodworking project.

People are so busy these days that they have very little time to stop and observe how things are made. Some assume that many of the items they purchase are made with the same quality of materials. Well, they're not. Most are made with the cheapest materials and not built to last, putting us in a situation of having to repurchase them over and over again.

Take a look at how this book is constructed. Its size is similar to that of a cookbook. Its binding allows it to lie flat on any surface, making the step-by-step instructions easy to follow. Its sturdy design will encourage you to bring it along to your work site, and to keep track of your progress in the note sections.

By learning the basic skills in this book, you will get the satisfaction of constructing something with your own hands.

Let me challenge you with this question: Why buy it, when you can build it yourself?

Safety in the Workspace

Before you start building, we first have to talk about safety.

Find a work area that is free from clutter and will give you enough space to move around in. Select a solid, flat work surface. **(fig. 1)** It can be an old tabletop on sawhorses, or something you build yourself. Keep in mind that you might drill and cut into it, so it should be a surface you can dedicate for this purpose. With every project, get into the routine of cleaning up after each step. This will give you a chance to review what you have accomplished and help you prepare for the next steps. Protect yourself by wearing safety glasses, ear protection, and dust protection. **(fig. 2)** Never wear loose-fitting clothing that could get caught on tools or workpieces. When building a project, the activity can be strenuous, almost like a workout, so work at a pace that is comfortable for you. When using hand and power tools, be aware of your surroundings, your balance, and where the tool may go if you lose control of it. Never reach over your work to screw or nail pieces together. Clean up after each work session and collect scraps in a bin; it can be as simple as tossing things in an old bucket.

Measuring and Marking

Find a ruler you feel comfortable using. It should fit nicely in your hand. I prefer a folding ruler, but this is a personal choice. **(fig. 3)** Sometimes the ruler finds the woodworker.

Pencils, pencils, and more pencils! **(fig. 4)** I keep at least five to ten pencils on hand since I break and lose them all the time. I find it helpful to include a drawing compass as well.

A try square is another essential woodworking tool. **(fig. 5)** You can use it to check for the accuracy of a right angle, mark locations, and transfer lines from one surface to another. I highly recommend adding one to your toolbox.

Another tool I frequently use is the steel square, more commonly referred to as the framing square. **(fig. 6)** I use it to keep larger projects square during assembly. It is not an essential tool to have, but it is very helpful.

Saws and Cutting

Sawing wood is probably the most challenging skill for most novice woodworkers to master. A great way to start is by learning how to use a backsaw and miter box. **(figs. 7–8)** The backsaw has a short reinforced blade that is easy to control and will produce precise cuts. The backsaw fits nicely into the slots of the miter box, which acts as a guide, keeping the saw in-line. Miter boxes haven't changed in three centuries. The simple wooden box design is still favored by carpenters today. By using these two tools together you will be able to make accurate cuts quickly and efficiently.

Some other useful tools that will help you hone your cutting skills are the coping saw and the hacksaw. **(figs. 9–10)** With a coping saw you will be able to cut intricate interior and exterior curves through different thicknesses of wood The hacksaw is most commonly used to cut through metal but is also great for cutting other materials like plastic and wood.

I would recommend familiarizing yourself with hand saws first before moving on to handheld power tools such as a jigsaw and circular saw. **(figs. 11–12)**

1
2
STANLEY
FatMax
30
3
4
5
6
7
8
9
10
11
PORTER+CABLE
12
13
14

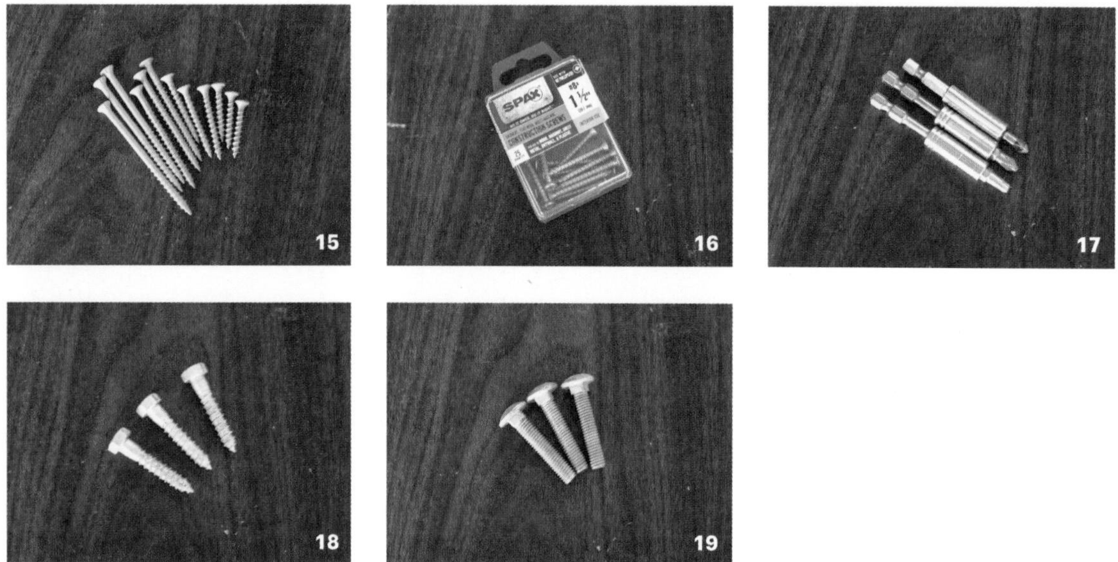
15 16 17 18 19

If you decide to use a power saw, then I would recommend the jigsaw. It is a versatile tool that will allow you to make crosscuts (cutting a piece of wood perpendicular to, or against, the wood grain) and rip cuts (cutting a piece of wood parallel to the grain); it can also cut curves and circles. Jigsaws are lightweight and relatively inexpensive, and can be purchased online or at garage sales. You will see in the step-by-step photos that I use the jigsaw quite a bit.

With any power tool, take the time to acquaint yourself with the tool and practice on scrap wood as much as possible, until you are comfortable with your particular model's functions and behavior.

Once you've made the decision to add larger and more powerful tools to your home workshop, a miter saw and table saw will be the most useful. **(figs. 13–14)** Both come in a variety of sizes and price points, and will add a layer of accuracy and speed to all of your projects.

Putting Projects Together

The most common method of connecting two pieces of wood is with screws and bolts. If you are a novice and have never used either before, the number of available products offered at home improvement centers can be both overwhelming and impressive.

Screws and bolts are not all made the same but they will do the same job. The question is, how long will a particular screw or bolt last? The kinds of screws and bolts you'll purchase are linked to the types of conditions your project will be exposed to. Will your project be indoors, outdoors, wet, dry, or somewhere in between?

Building a project that will be exposed to wet conditions for an extended period of time requires a specific type of screw. The best choice is the deck screw. **(fig. 15)** These screws are coated in ceramic, which prevents them from rusting, and are designed with a special tip to help guide them into the wood.

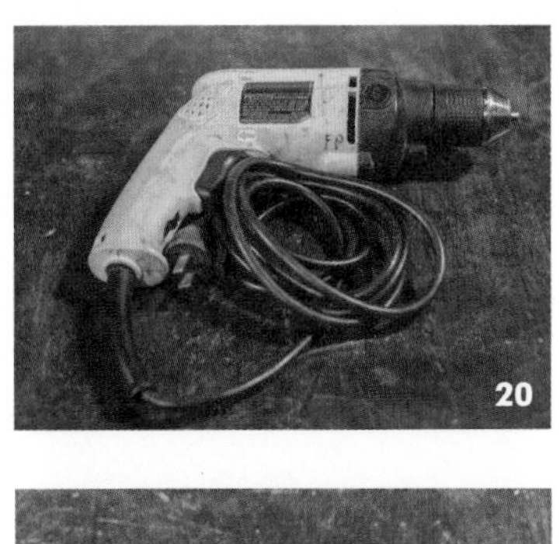
20

21

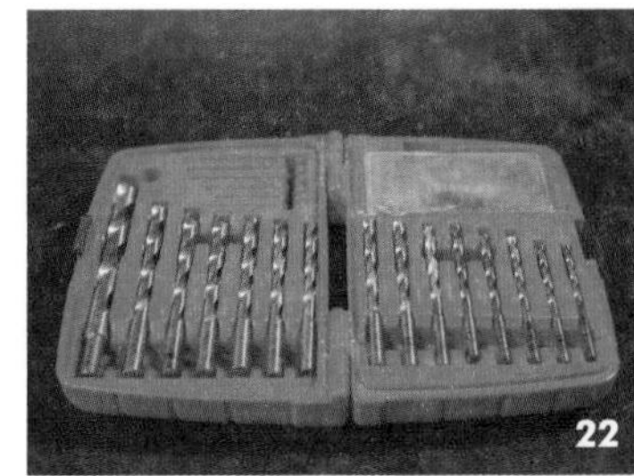
22

23

24

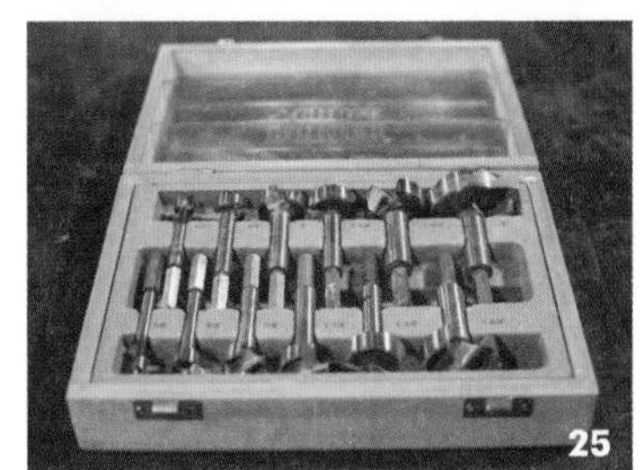
25

Another screw that I have selected is the SPAX brand construction screw. **(fig. 16)** These screws are "heat treated," a process that adds hardness, strength, and durability. They come in a brass finish that gives projects a polished look.

The easiest and most efficient way to install these screws is with a cordless drill fitted with a magnetic tip holder. **(fig. 17)**

When connecting larger pieces of wood together, galvanized lag screws and carriage bolts are a great choice. **(figs. 18–19)** Galvanizing is a process of coating iron and steel with zinc oxide, which gives them a layer of protection against damp conditions.

Before installing these screws, you will have to predrill your piece of wood. Predrilling is when you drill a hole to accommodate the diameter of the screw you are installing.

All of these fasteners are available in a wide variety of sizes and thicknesses.

Drills: Corded and Cordless

Both corded and cordless drills work fine. **(figs. 20–21)** Battery-operated drills have the advantage of mobility, but run out of power after a short period of time. Corded drills never run out of power, but have a tethered wire. Corded drills are also significantly more powerful, and should be used with caution. I would recommend using a cordless drill at first, before moving on to a corded drill. Just make sure whichever drill you choose, it is a variable speed drill. These will utilize the drill's trigger to vary its speed in revolutions per minute (rpms)—the more you depress the trigger, the faster the drill will go. A fast speed is perfect for drilling holes; slower speeds are best for attaching pieces together with screws.

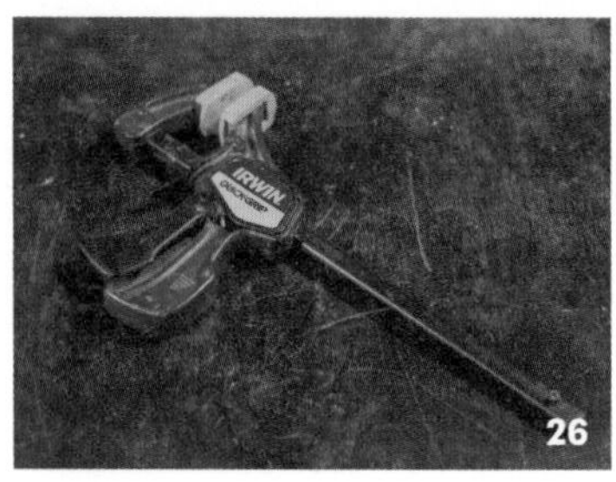

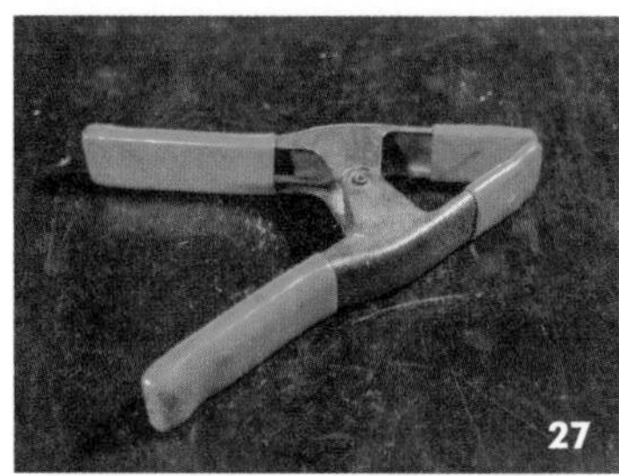

Drilling and Countersinking

I think everyone should own a drill bit set. **(fig. 22)** They are available at any hardware or home store. The most common sizes are ⁵⁄₃₂" through ½". When using mechanical fasteners (screws), I prefer to predrill most holes, because widening the hole makes the wood less likely to split when you're driving a screw into it. (It's important to note that predrilling past the length of your screw will weaken the connection, since there is less material for the screw to bite into.) I usually follow with a countersinking bit. Countersink bits are used to allow the head of the screw to sit flush or slightly below the surface of the wood. **(fig. 23)** If you countersink the screw below the wood, the space you created can be filled with wood filler. Wood filler, also known as plastic wood, comes in a wide variety of pigments. **(fig. 24)** It can come in handy if you're looking for a really polished look to your piece. You can fill the holes and paint or varnish your projects.

On some of these projects, when I needed to drill a larger hole, I used a Forstner bit. **(fig. 25)** This is a type of flat-bottom bit, which cuts through wood leaving a clean and precise hole. A set of these bits can be expensive but each bit can also be purchased individually.

Clamps

Clamps are a big part of every woodworker's tool box and an important tool to ensure your safety in your workspace, but it's up to you to make them part of your woodworking routine. They act as another set of hands. I use them to secure project pieces to my work surface. This helps to prevent pieces of wood from becoming projectiles when drilling or cutting. Clamps come in a wide variety of types, sizes, and styles. I like to use quick-release clamps and spring clamps. **(figs. 26–27)** They are very popular because of their one-handed operation, but any clamp that will hold pieces of wood together will work.

Backer Boards

When drilling, I recommend using a backer board. **(fig. 28)** It will prevent you from drilling into your work surface and help stop the potential for tear-out on project pieces. Tear-out can occur anytime you drill or cut into wood. The wood fibers tear away from the edges of the area being cut or drilled into. Backer boards extend the area being cut and will minimize this type of damage.

Introduction to Wood

Before selecting wood for a project, you have to ask yourself the following questions: Is this my first woodworking project? How much experience do I have building things? Do I want to invest a lot of time and money? Will this project be used indoors or outdoors? Should I stain or paint the finished piece?

If you need help answering these questions, this book will take the guesswork out of wood selection. Finding something to build is easy, but figuring out what to purchase for it can take a lot of time and effort. To help you speed up this process, I have selected materials that are easy to work with and can be found in any home improvement center.

Pine

Pine boards come in a variety of species, sizes, and grades. Pine's soft texture and straight grain make it one of the easiest woods to work with. Relatively inexpensive, it's a perfect selection for someone new to woodworking and on a fixed budget. While pine may have a reputation as a construction material, when used for our purposes, it can yield some fantastic results. I use it exclusively in all of my classes.

The most common species of wood are sugar pine, western white pine, eastern white pine, and radiata pine. Sugar pine (*Pinus lambertiana*) is harvested in mountainous regions on the Pacific Coast of the United States. Light brown in color with a slight reddish hue, it has a medium to coarse texture with a straight and even grain. Sugar pine releases a sweet odor when worked on, both with hand and power tools.

Western white pine (*Pinus monticola*) is harvested in the mountainous regions of western North America. Its color is a light brown that has a tendecy to darken with age. It has a medium texture with a straight and even grain. Western white pine emits a faintly resinous odor while being worked, and will glue and finish well.

Eastern white pine (*Pinus strobus*) is harvested in eastern North America. It is light brown in color with a tinge of red, and has a medium texture with a straight and even grain. Eastern white pine gives off a mild resinous odor while being worked, and will glue and finish well.

Radiata pine (*Pinus radiata*) is harvested in the central and southern coastal region of California, as well as throughout the southern hemisphere, where it is widely planted. Its heartwood is light brown, while its wide sapwood is yellowish white. Radiata pine has a medium, even texture, a straight grain, and is knot free. It produces a light resinous odor while being worked, and will glue and finish well.

All species of pine come in different grades, which are based on appearance, strength, and work ability, as outlined in the following chart.

GRADES OF SOFTWOODS

Grade	Description
C Select	Used for interior trims and cabinets. Completely clear of defects.
D Select	May have dimed-sized knots. Nearly clear of defects.
#1 Common	Will have tight knots that will be generally small in size. Best material for pine with a knotty look.
#2 Common	Has tight knots larger than those found in #1 Common. Best for woodworking projects.

Framing Lumber

Framing lumber, sometimes referred to as dimensional lumber, is the standard material used in construction. I use this lumber to build worktables, potting benches, trellises, and shelf units. You will see it stacked up high on racks labeled as 2×4's, 2×6's, 2×12's, etc. It's important to know that this type of wood is part of a larger group of species called SPF, which is a collection of spruce, pine, and fir, and will be found mixed together in the same stack.

The most important thing you will have to consider when purchasing this type of wood is its moisture content. It is available in two types: S-Green and S-Dry. S-Green has over 19 percent water weight and can shrink or warp if used undried. S-Dry has less than 19 percent water weight and can be used immediately.

The first thing you will need to learn before purchasing any pine or framing lumber is the labeling system developed by the lumber mills. How this system came to be is irrelevant. All you need to know is how to translate it.

Did you know that a two-by-four (2×4) doesn't actually measure two inches (2") by four inches (4")? Well, if you answered no, don't feel bad. When I started in woodworking, I also would have answered no. All the measurements you'll find for pine and lumber are "nominal" measurements—in name only. The "actual" dimensions are the real measurements of wood after the drying and planning process.

So before you start any project you will need to convert these measurements using two scales: the inch and quarter scales. See the charts below.

Moldings

Incorporating moldings into your projects will give you access to material you might not be able to cut yourself. The variety of styles and types will be a great resource. Priced by the linear foot and labeled using "actual" dimensions, this material requires very little sanding or prep work. Most home improvement centers will either cut lengths for you or have cutting stations. By using this material, you will save a lot of time and money.

Before you start any of these projects, let me give you a few tips on what to look out for when you select wood.

INCH SCALE

Nominal Size	Actual Size
1×2"	¾" × 1 ½"
1×3"	¾" × 2 ½"
1×4"	¾" × 3 ½"
1×5"	¾" × 4 ½"
1×6"	¾" × 5 ½"
1×8"	¾" × 7 ¼"
1×10"	¾" × 9 ¼"
1×12"	¾" × 11 ¼"

QUARTER SCALE

Nominal Size	Actual Size
5/4×6"	1 (⅛)" × 5 ½"
6/4×6"	1 (⅜)" × 5 ½"
8/4×6"	1 (13/16)" × 5 ½"
12/4×6"	2 (13/16)" × 5 ½"
16/4×6"	3 (13/16)" × 5 ½"

How to Select the Best Piece of Wood

STEP 1

Always bring a tape measure.

Never assume the measurements listed are correct.

STEP 2

Learn how to inspect wood.

The best way to do this is by doing a visual inspection. Following are nine of the most common defects you will find when selecting a piece of wood.

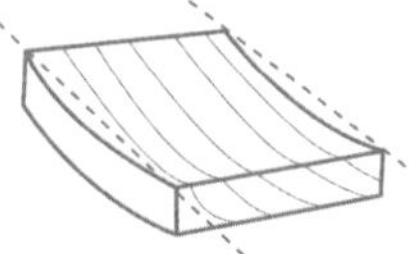

1. BOW
A warp on the face of a board from end to end

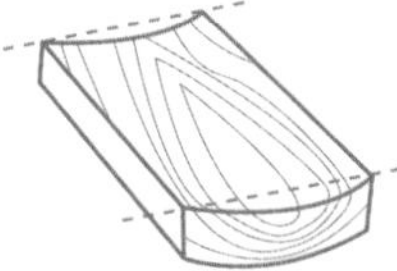

2. CUP
A hollow across the face of a board

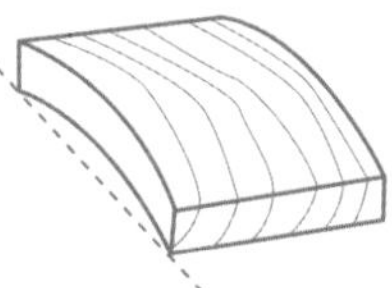

3. CROOK
A warp along the edge line; also known as a crown

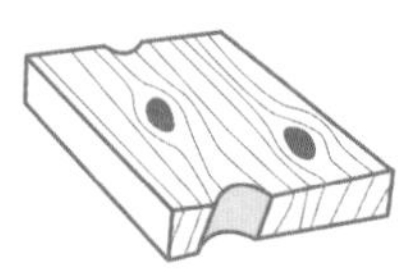

4. KNOT or KNOTHOLE
A tight knot is usually not a problem; a loose or dead knot, surrounded by a dark ring, may fall out or may have already left a hole

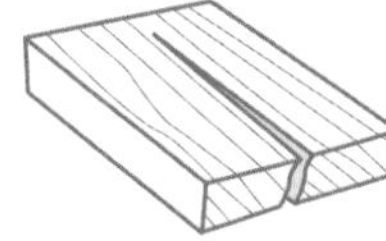

5. SPLIT
A crack going all the way through the piece of wood, commonly at the ends

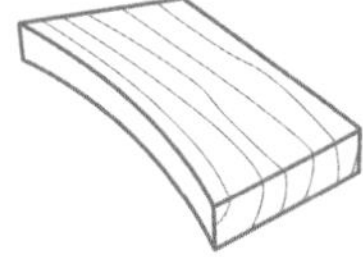

6. TWIST
Multiple bends in a board

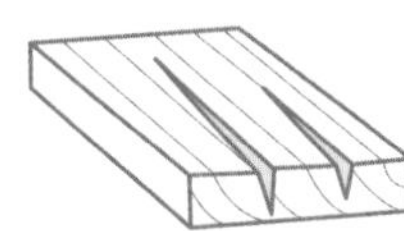

7. CHECK
A crack along the wood's annual growth rings, not passing through the entire thickness of the wood

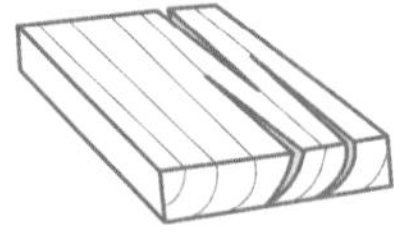

8. SHAKE
Separation of grain between the growth rings, often extending along the board's face, and sometimes below its surface

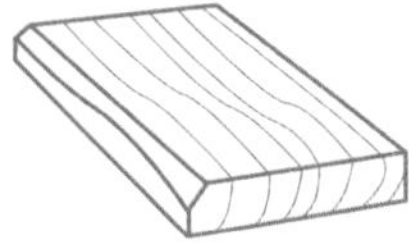

9. WANE
Missing wood or untrimmed bark along the edge or corner of the piece

STEP 3

Try to purchase all of your wood from the same stack.

A newly opened stack would be even better. Home improvement centers generally get different species of the same wood and mix them together as the shipments overlap.

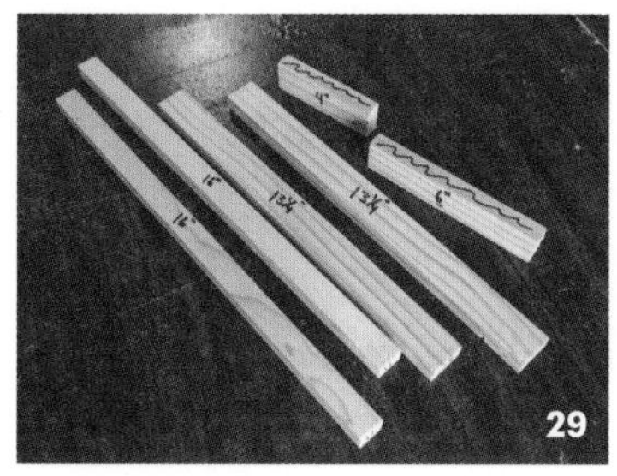
29

30

31

Finishing Your Project

When it comes to finishing your project, here are two options I would recommend:

Option 1. **PAINT**

You first need to determine whether you plan on using this project indoors or outdoors, which will make a big difference when you're selecting your paint. I prefer using water-based paints and inexpensive chip brushes to avoid safety issues and enable easy cleanup. You should get advice from a paint store or home improvement center, where someone can guide you when it comes to making those choices. When prepping your project, you should fill any screw holes and voids with wood filler. Let it dry overnight, and apply a second coat if needed. Sand the entire project with two types of sandpaper—a medium grit first, then a fine grit. Clean the surface, dusting with a damp cloth or paper towel. Apply two coats of primer, letting each coat dry overnight, before applying an even coat of finish paint. In some cases, the primer may bleed through and you will need to apply a second coat.

Option 2. **VARNISH OR POLYURETHANE**

If you want to give your project a clear finished look, then varnish and polyurethane are both great products. But be warned: when applying these finishes, you will need to take some precautionary steps to ensure your safety and health. In this case, definitely get advice from a paint store or home improvement center. They can suggest different finishes and help you with the safety equipment you will need. Once you have selected the type of finish you want, you will need to set up a dedicated space that is clean and dust free. It should be a place where you can leave your project undisturbed for an extended period of time. Practice first by applying your finish on a piece of scrap wood and leave it to dry overnight. Sand the piece with fine-grit sandpaper and clean off any residue with a rag and mineral spirits. You may need to apply multiple coats to get the desired finish you want.

Thinking Outside the Box

I am always looking for easier and more efficient ways to build projects. I like to use what I call "memory sticks." These are pieces of wood that are cut to specific lengths and help to mark locations of screws or the spacing of project parts. **(fig. 29)** They eliminate the need to constantly measure with a ruler. If I design a project that has a lot of rounded edges, I like to trace the edges with a piece of plastic pipe.

(fig. 30) For a larger circumference, I might use a paint can. **(fig. 31)** When I'm building prototypes for projects, I may get stuck and have to search for a completely different type of material. What I like to do is go to a home improvement center and search every aisle until I see something that will spark an idea. It's always something I would have never thought about using. Some great examples are the fluorescent lightbulb tubes that I used for the birdfeeder, and the rebar and conduit clamps on the garden fence. **(fig. 32)** When I use these objects, projects become more creative and interesting. You will be surprised by how many items from different trades are available and will work together.

Woodworking Jigs

A great way to speed up the assembly process of any project is to use jigs. When I teach my classes, the students are amazed at the different types of jigs we use to build. I use them to align pieces together, to aid with drilling and space, or to complete a repetitive task. I have also built full projects only using jigs. My students are always surprised that they don't always need to use a ruler. If you've never used or seen a jig before, they look like small wooden tools. Most are made from scrap pieces or cutoffs, so always keep these pieces on hand; you never know when you might need them. I have included above and throughout this book plans and photographs of my most frequently used jigs.

The "T" Jig

This is a double-sided jig used to predrill consistent holes on the ends of boards. **(fig. 33)**

Featured in the Garden Table and Garden Chair projects.

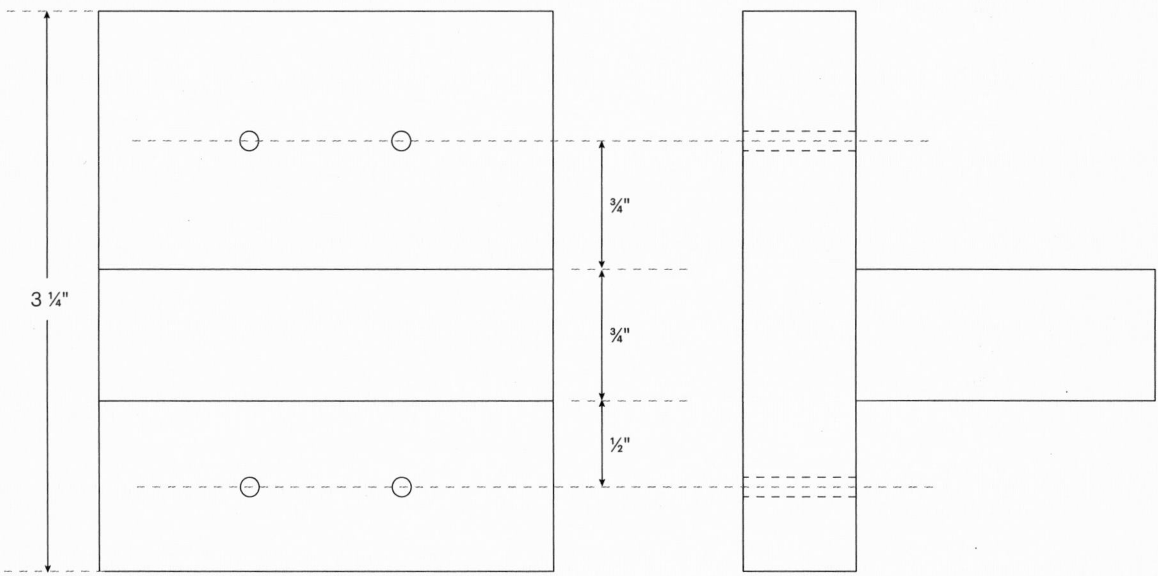

The "Attaching" Jig

This jig is used to lock two pieces of wood together at a 90-degree angle. **(fig. 34)**

Featured in the Cold Frame project.

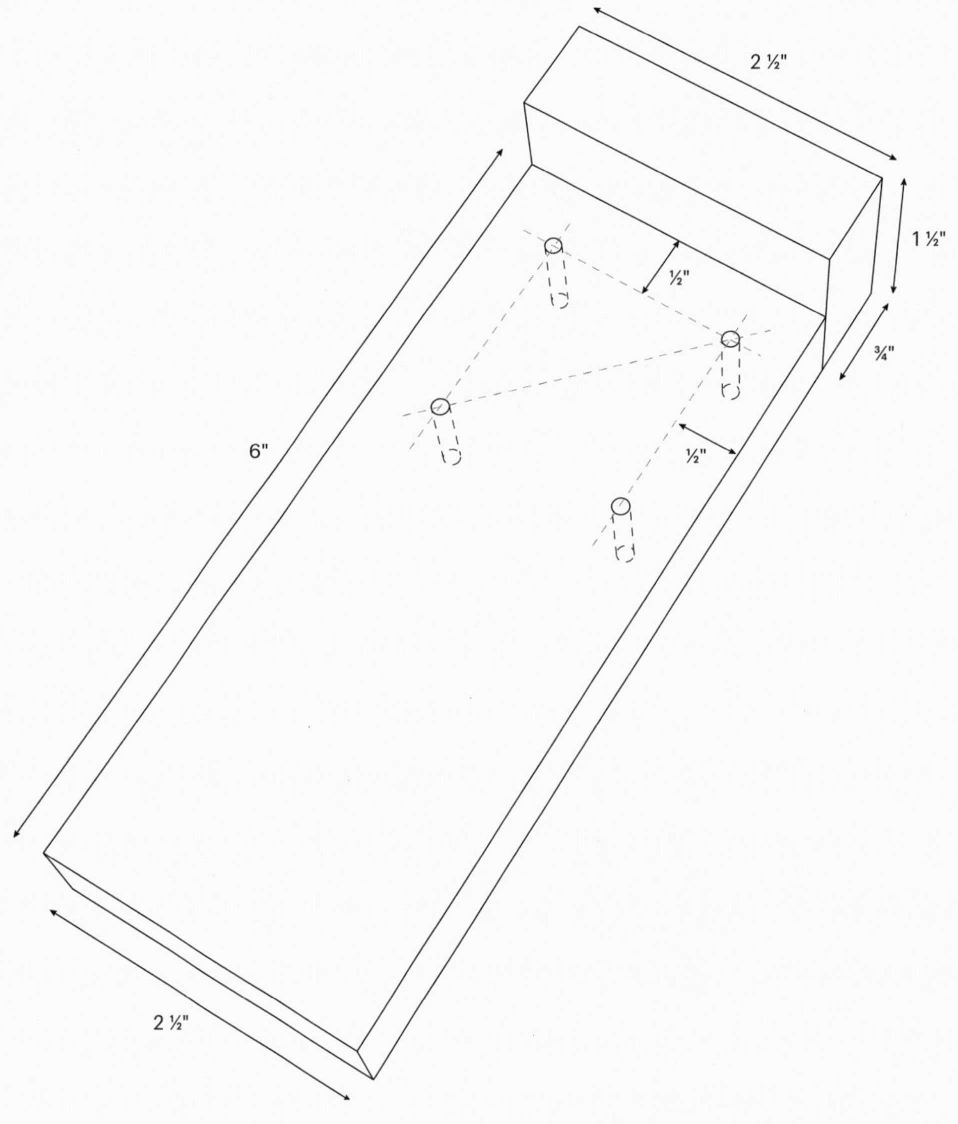

The "Centering" Jig

This jig is used to find the center of a dowel.
(fig. 35)

Featured in the Harvest Basket project.

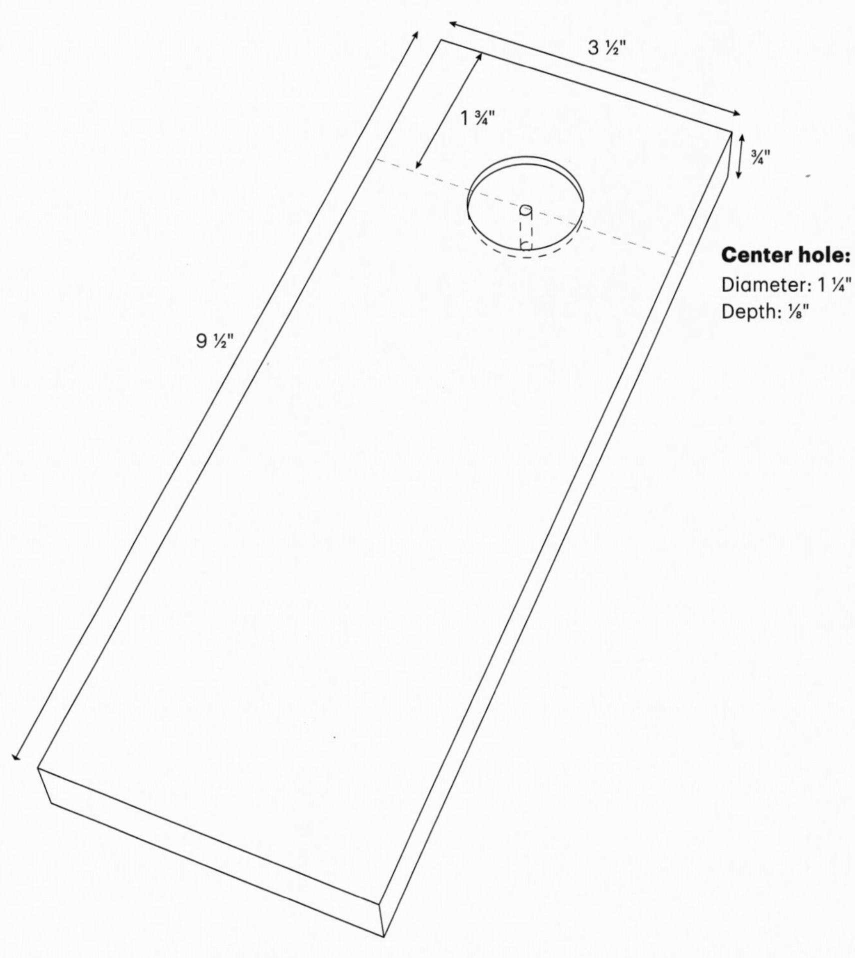

The "Backer Stacker"

This jig has a dual purpose: it's a backer board and a wood stacker. **(fig. 36)**

Featured in the Harvest Basket and Plant Stand projects.

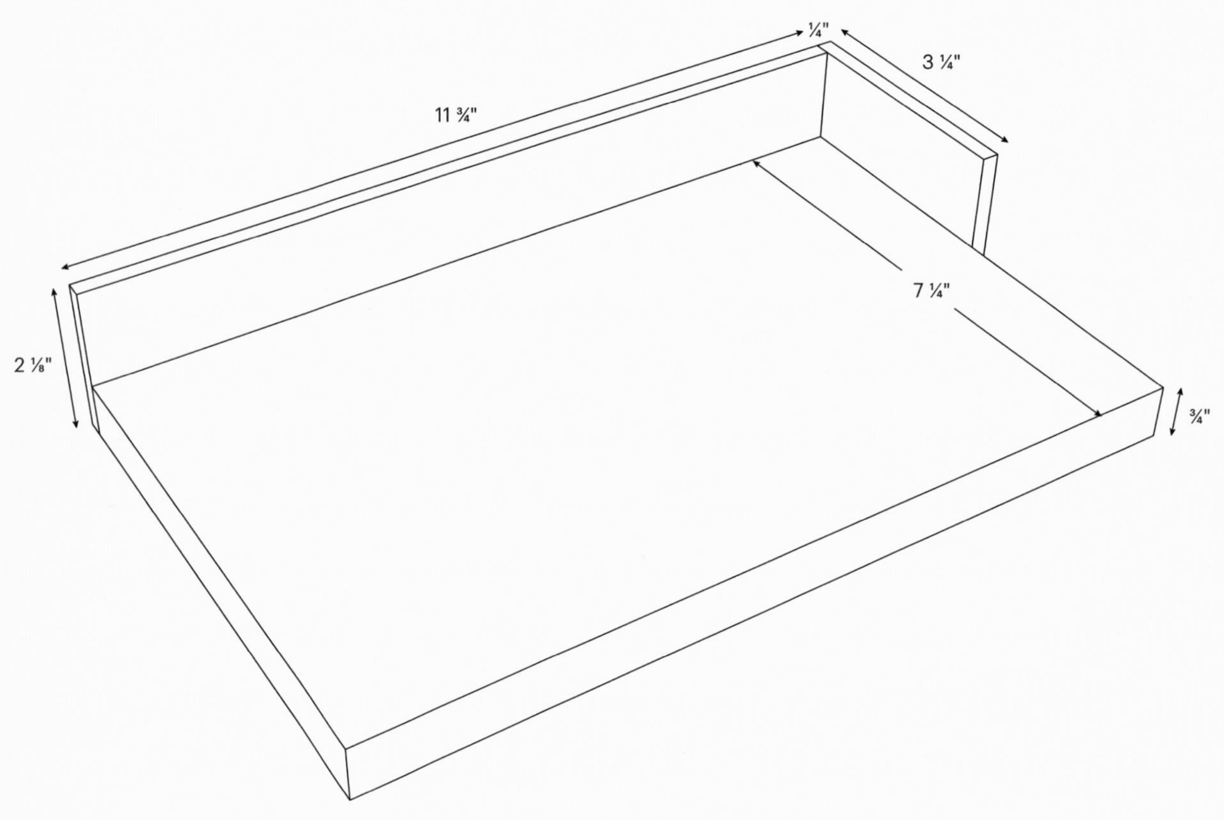

The "Angle" Jig

This jig is used to find different angles within the same project. **(fig. 37)**

Featured in the Garden Chair project.

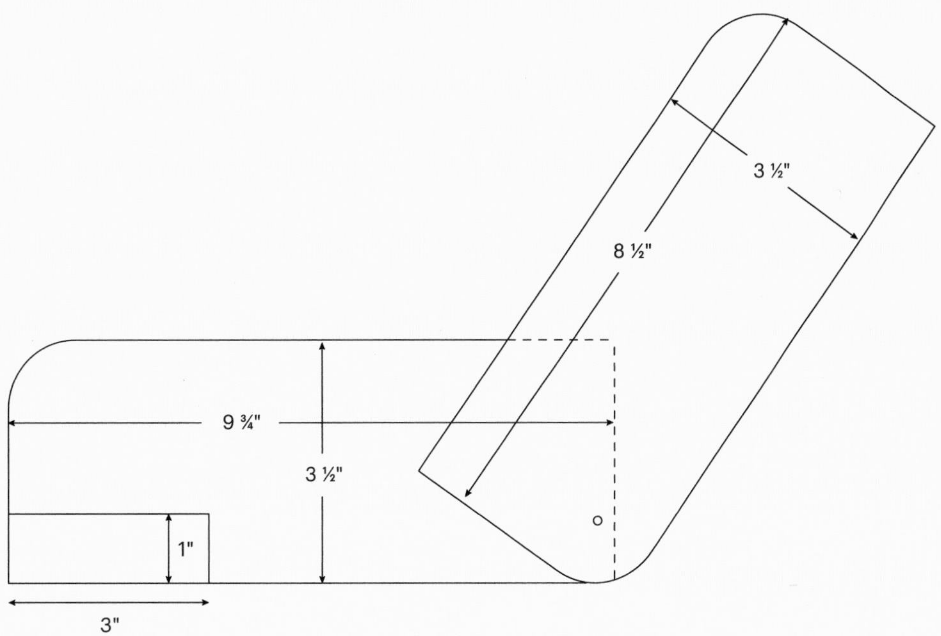

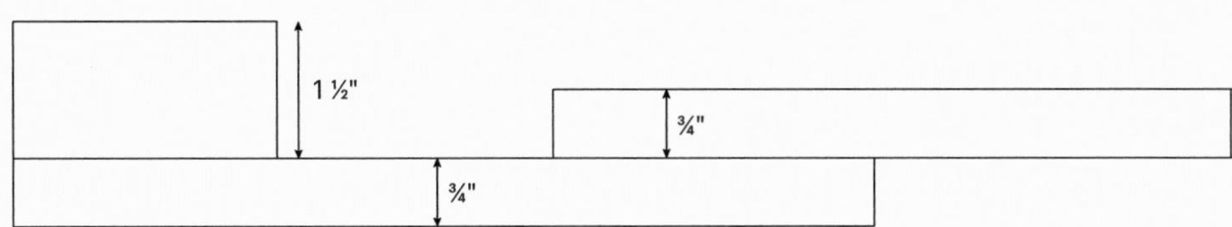

Projects

1.

Harvest Basket

Sometimes referred to as a "garden hod," the harvest basket conjures images of a farming community working together to gather crops. Take it with you for outdoor chores like picking fruits and vegetables; a quick rinse with a hose or tap and excess water drains right out of the bottom. Keep one indoors as a catchall for magazines, mail, and fruits. Recently, I have been using the basket in my kitchen as a planter for herbs and spices.

Materials Needed

HARDWARE:

- (8) 1 ½" brass-plated wood screws
- (20) #8 × ¾" brass-plated wood screws
- (1) sheet of 80-grit sandpaper
- (1) sheet of 220-grit sandpaper

TOOLS:

- Pencil
- Try square
- Straight edge
- Phillips-head screwdriver
- Tape measure
- Compass
- Cordless screw gun or corded drill
- #6 countersink drill bit
- Magnetic tip holder with a #2 Phillips insert bit
- ⅛" drill bit
- ½" drill bit
- 1 ¼" Forstner bit
- Miter saw or miter box (optional)
- Table saw (optional)
- Jigsaw or coping saw (optional)

Diagram A
Materials & Cutting

A Sides (2): ¾" × 10" × 10"
B Bottom: ¾" × 5 ¼" × 14 ½"
C Slats (10): ¼" × ⅞" × 16"
Dowel (not shown): 1 ¼" Ø × 14 ½"

1" × 10" × 96" — Knotted Pine

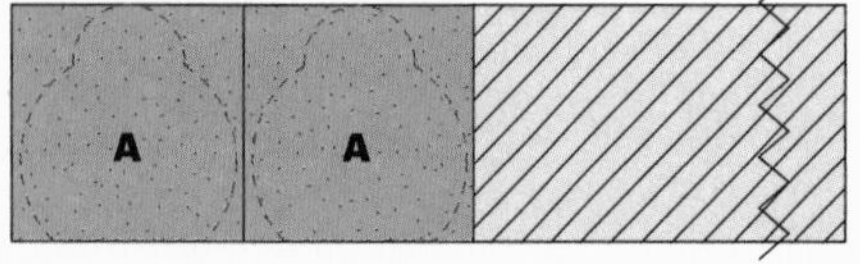

1" × 6" × 96" — Knotted Pine

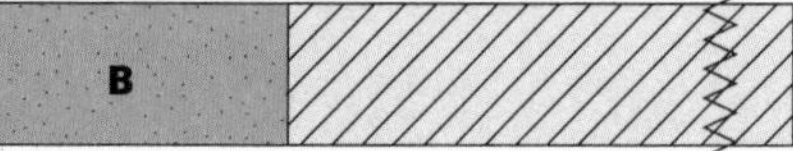

C ¼" × ⅞" × 96" — Prefinished Pine Moldings

Used as slat/spacer template

Diagram B

Diagram C

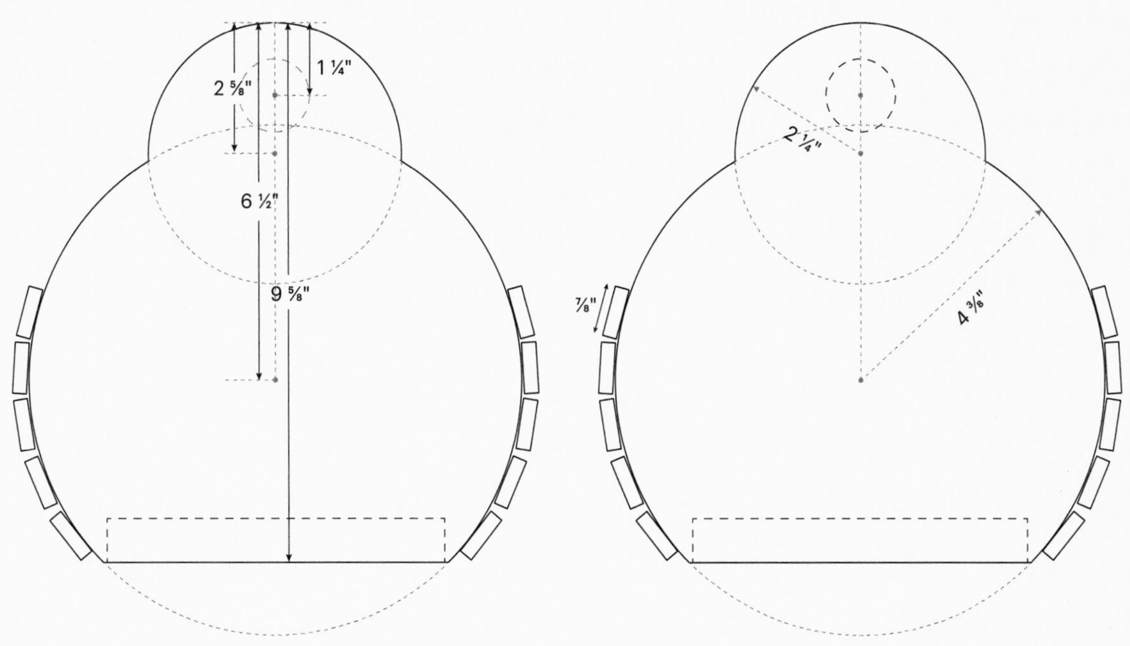

Diagram D

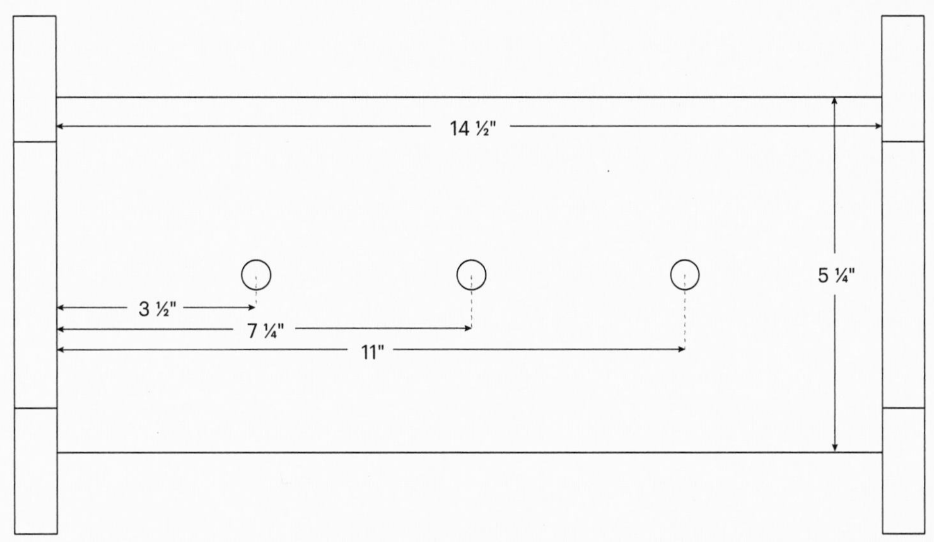

STEP 1

Building the Sides

Select a piece of 1" × 10" × 8' knotted pine. Crosscut it into two 10" long pieces and label both pieces "side."

STEP 2

Making a Centerline

Take both sidepieces and measure and scribe marks on each end at 4 ⅝". Use the straight edge to connect the marks. **(fig. 1)**

Use the try square to continue the centerlines on to the opposite sides as shown in **figure 2**.

STEP 3

Laying Out the Handle

Measure along the centerlines and scribe marks at 1 ¼". Take the #6 countersink bit and drill on the marks. **(fig. 3)**

STEP 4

Laying Out the Sides

Measure along the centerlines and scribe marks at 2 ⅝". Use the compass to draw 4 ½" diameter circles on the marks. Measure along the centerlines and scribe marks at 6 ½". Use the compass to draw 8 ¾" diameter circles on the marks. Measure along the centerlines and scribe marks at 9 ⅝". Use the try square to draw lines across the marks, then measure and mark at 2 ¼" on both sides of the centerlines. Take the #6 countersink bit and drill on the marks. **(fig. 4)**

STEP 5

Cutting the Sides

Using the jigsaw or coping saw, cut along the lines. **(fig. 5)**

Using a piece of 80-grit sandpaper, sand and shape the sides. Use a piece of 220-grit sandpaper to smooth the surfaces. **(fig. 6)**

STEP 6

Building the Bottom

Select a piece of 1" × 6" × 8' knotted pine. Crosscut one 14 ½" long piece and label it "bottom."

1
2
3
4
5
6
7
8

STEP 7

Making a Centerline

Take the bottom piece and measure and scribe marks at 2 ⅝" on each end. Use the straight edge to connect the marks. **(fig. 7)**

Measure along the centerline, scribing marks at 3 ½", 7 ¼", and 11". Place a piece of scrap wood underneath the bottom piece. Using the ½" bit, drill through the marks. **(fig. 8)**

STEP 8

Making the Dowel Handle

Cut a piece of 1 ¼" dowel to 14 ½" long.

STEP 9

Making the Slats

Select two pieces of ¼" × ⅞" × 8' pine and crosscut them into eleven 16" long pieces.

HELPFUL HINT: The pieces for the slats are prefinished pine moldings that you can find at any hardware or home improvement store.

STEP 10

Making the Slat/Spacer Template

Take a slat and measure and scribe a mark at ⅜". Use the try square to draw a line across the mark. Measure along the line and mark it at 7⁄16". Take the slat and place a piece of scrap wood underneath it. Using the ⅛" bit, drill through the mark. **(fig. 9)**

STEP 11

Predrilling the Slats

Take the slat/spacer template and position it on top of two slats. Place a piece of scrap wood underneath and, with the ⅛" drill bit, drill through all of the pieces. Repeat with the remaining slats.

Place a piece of scrap wood underneath the predrilled slats. Using the #6 countersink bit, drill into each slat. **(figs. 10 & 12)**

HELPFUL HINT: Use the backer stacker jig to keep your slats aligned and prevent tear-out during drilling. (**fig. 11**; see page 26)

Using a piece of 220-grit sandpaper, sand and slightly round the edges of the slats.

STEP 12

Finding the Center of the Dowel

To create a centering jig, use the 1 ¼" Forstner bit to drill a ½" deep hole into a piece of scrap wood. (See page 25.) Take the ⅛" bit and drill through the center point of the hole. **(fig. 13)**

Take the dowel handle and place it into the 1 ¼" hole. Using the ⅛" bit, drill a 1" deep hole into the dowel. **(fig. 14)**

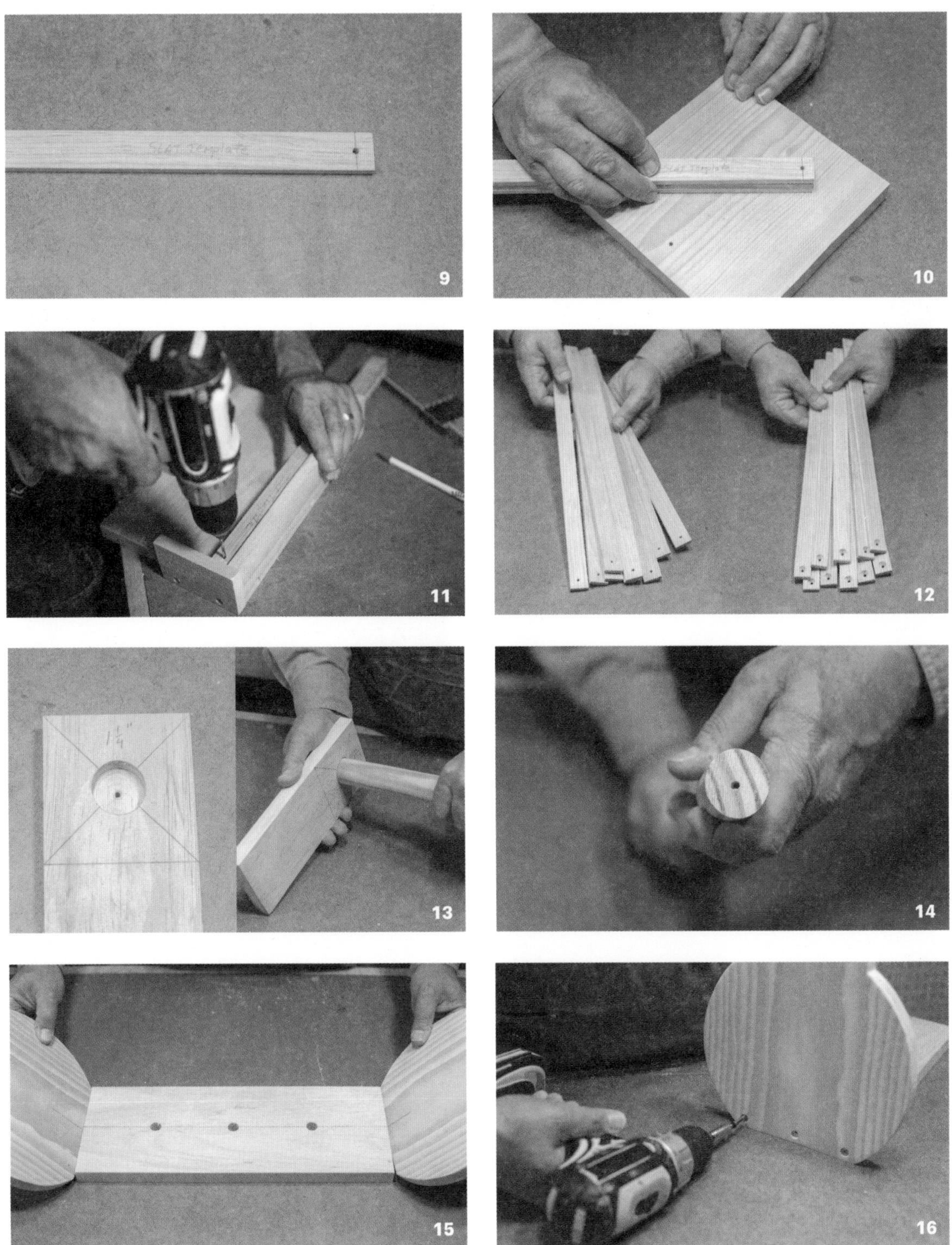

17
18
19
20
21
22
23

STEP 13

Attaching the Sides to the Bottom

Use the centerlines to align the bottom and sidepieces. **(fig. 15)**

Predrill the holes using the ⅛" drill bit. Using the #2 Phillips bit, insert six 1 ½" wood screws into the holes. **(figs. 16–17)**

STEP 14

Attaching the Handle

Using the #2 Phillips bit, insert two 1 ½" wood screws into the holes, letting the tips of the screws protrude slightly out of the sides. **(fig. 18)**

Align the dowel with the tips of the screws. Using the #2 Phillips bit, join the pieces. **(figs. 19–20)**

STEP 15

Attaching the Slats

Starting at the bottom, use a piece of scrap wood to align the first slat. **(fig. 21)**

Predrill the holes using the ⅛" drill bit. Use the screwdriver to insert the #8 × ¾" wood screws. **(fig. 22)**

As shown in **figure 23**, use the slat/spacer template and repeat the instructions to attach the remaining slats.

NOTES

2.

Garden Stool / Toolbox

Whether you're busy in the garden or fixing a car, this multipurpose stool will make the job easier. When you're working for long periods of time, sitting more frequently will lessen your chances of back and knee injury. Pull up the convenient handle when transporting tools to reduce the number of trips you need to make to your garage or toolshed.

Materials Needed

HARDWARE:

(1) 1 lb. box of 1 ¼" deck screws

(1) 1 lb. box of 1 ½" deck screws

(6) #8 x ¾" lath screws

(1) piece of 1 ½" diameter PVC pipe (2"–3" long)

(2) sheets of 220-grit sandpaper

TOOLS:

Pencil

Phillips-head screwdriver

Tape measure

Clamps

Ruler

Waterproof wood glue

Jigsaw or coping saw

Cordless screw gun or corded drill

#6 countersink drill bit

Magnetic tip holder with a #2 Phillips insert bit

2" Forstner bit

⅛" drill bit

½" drill bit

Miter saw or miter box (optional)

Table saw (optional)

Diagram A
Materials & Cutting

1" × 12" × 96" — Knotted Pine

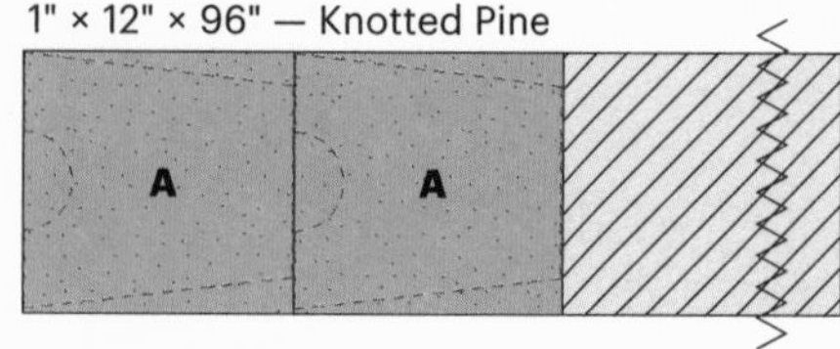

A Legs (2): ¾" × 11 ¼" × 12"
B Top (3): ¾" × 3 ½" × 16"
C Rails (2): ¾" × 2 ½" × 12 ¼"
D Handle: ¾" × 3 ½" × 12"
E Handle stopper: ¼" × 2" × 6"
F Tray bottom: ¼" × 9 ½" × 12 ¼"
G Cleats (2): ¾" × 1 ½" × 7 ½"

1" × 4" × 96" — Knotted Pine

¼" × 24" × 48" — Luan Plywood

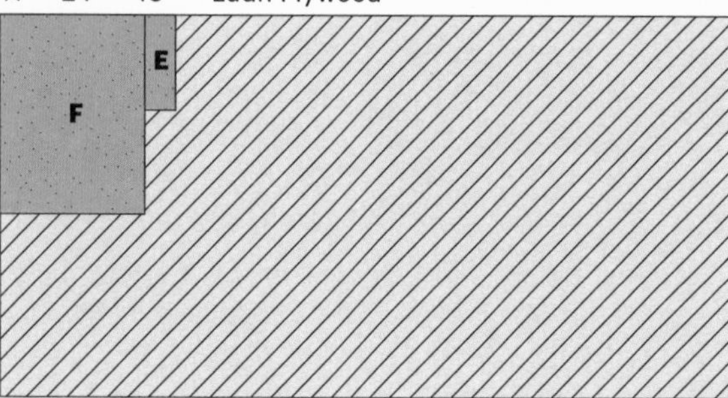

Diagram B
Handle

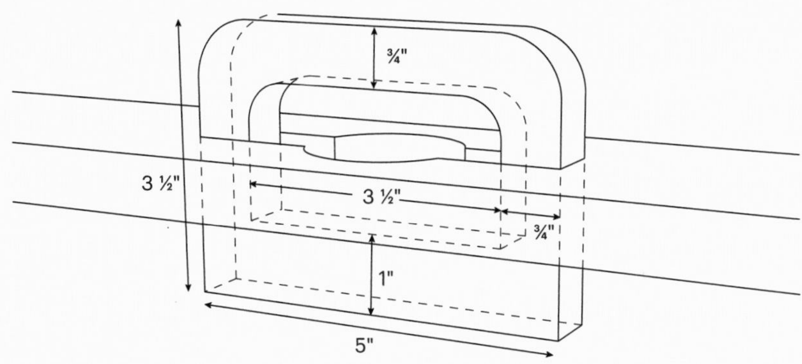

Diagram C
Top

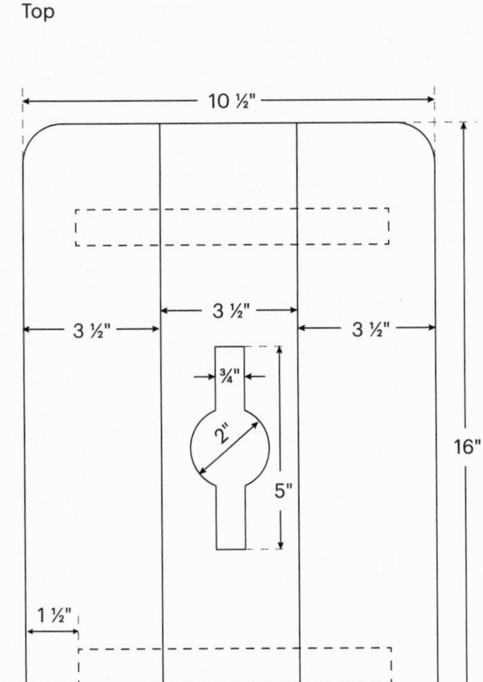

Diagram D
Side

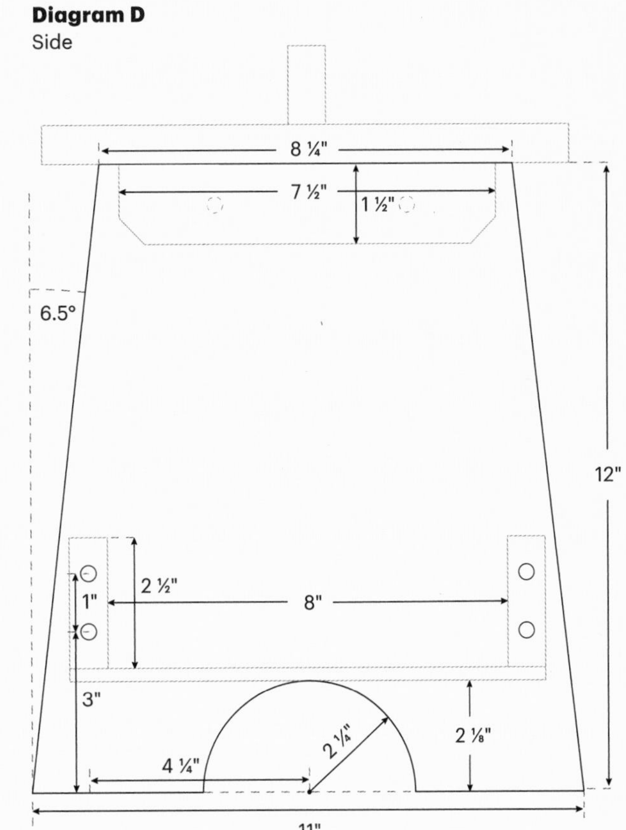

STEP 1

Making the Handle Opening

Select and cut a piece of pine measuring ¾" × 3 ½" × 16".

Using the pencil and ruler, draw the location of the handle opening as shown in **diagram C**.

Using a drill with the 2" Forstner bit, drill a hole through the center of the board. **(fig. 1)**

Cut along the layout lines with the jigsaw or coping saw. **(figs. 2–3)**

> **HELPFUL HINT:** To prevent tear-out when drilling, secure a piece of scrap wood under your workpiece.

STEP 2

Making the Top

Select and cut two pieces of pine, each measuring ¾" × 3 ½" × 16". Glue these pieces to the handle-opening piece. **(fig. 4)**

> **HELPFUL HINT:** To get a stronger bond between the boards, use a brush to spread the wood glue.

Use a clamp to secure the boards together. **(fig. 5)**

STEP 3

Making and Attaching the Cleats

Select and cut two pieces of pine, each measuring ¾" × 1 ½" × 7 ½".

Position and glue each cleat to the top as shown in **diagram C**, then secure each one by countersinking and attaching with 1 ¼" deck screws. **(fig. 6)**

Use a damp cloth to remove any excess glue that squeezes out. **(fig. 7)**

> **HELPFUL HINT:** For a finished look, trim off the edges of the attaching cleats.

Using the piece of 1 ½" PVC pipe, trace a line at each corner of the top. Cut along the lines using the jigsaw or coping saw. **(fig. 8)**

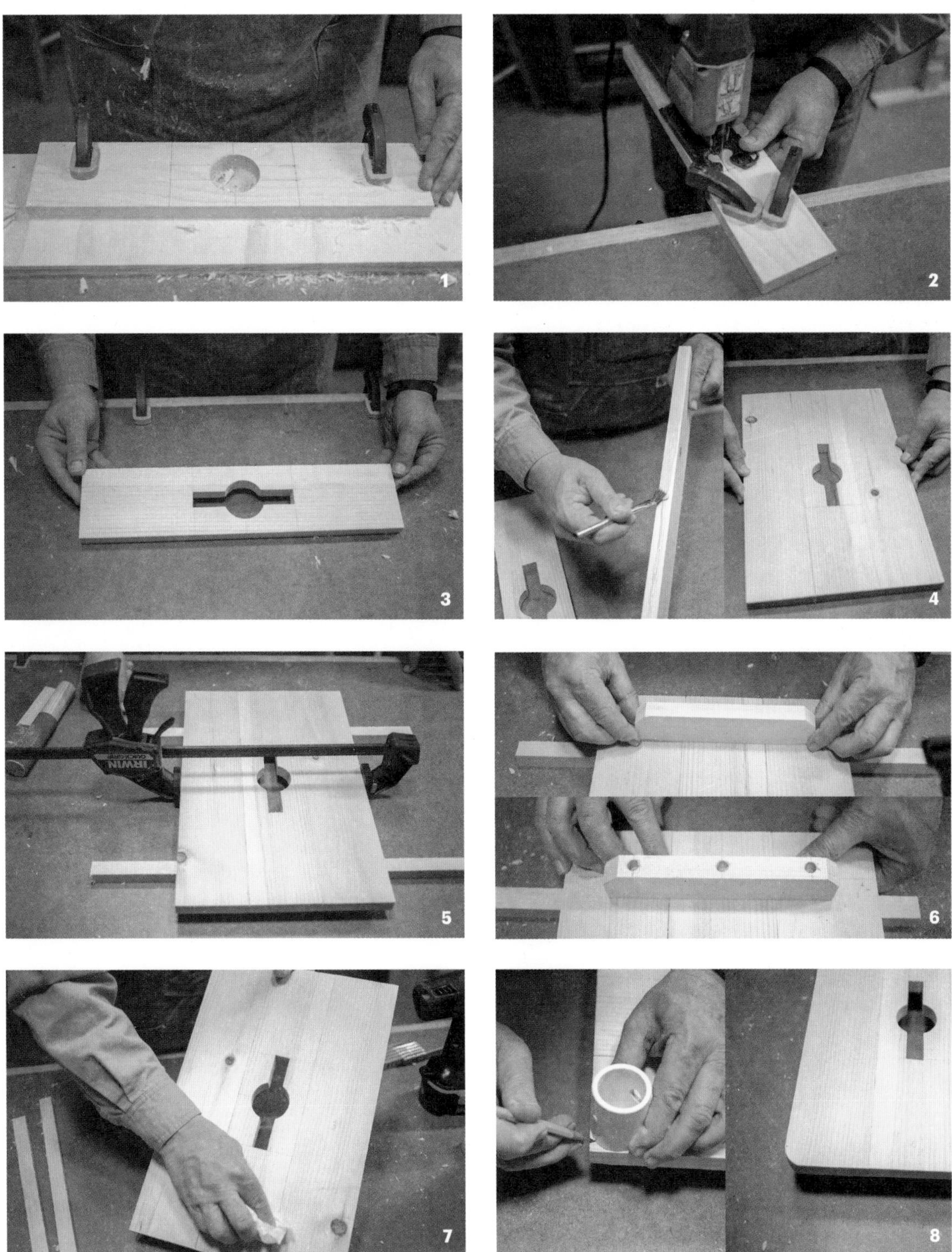
1
2
3
4
IRWIN
5
6
7
8

STEP 4

Making the Sides and Legs

Select and cut two pieces of pine, each measuring ¾" × 11 ¼" × 12".

Lay out the lines as shown in **diagram D**. **(fig. 9)**

As shown in **figure 10**, use a quart can to trace a circle at the bottom edge of the board, creating the legs.

Using the jigsaw or coping saw, cut along the lines. **(fig. 11)**

STEP 5

Attaching the Legs

As shown in **figure 12**, use clamps to hold the sidepieces to the cleats.

Attach the legs to the cleats by countersinking and screwing with 1 ¼" deck screws. **(figs. 13–14)**

HELPFUL HINT: Although it's nice to have a handle on the stool, you can build it without one.

STEP 6

Making the Handle

Select and cut a piece of pine measuring ¾" × 3 ½" × 12".

HELPFUL HINT: When working with small parts of a project, it is safer to leave the workpiece up to two-thirds longer than specified. This will help to secure the piece while cutting.

Lay out the lines for the handle (see **diagram B**), using the piece of PVC pipe to create the rounded shape as shown in **figure 15**.

Secure the workpiece with clamps and drill four ½" holes in the handle. **(fig. 16)**

Using the jigsaw or coping saw, cut the handle along the layout lines. **(figs. 17–18)**

Using sandpaper, shape the handle. **(figs. 19–20)**

Take the finished handle and test fit it into the top. Adjust as needed. **(fig. 21)**

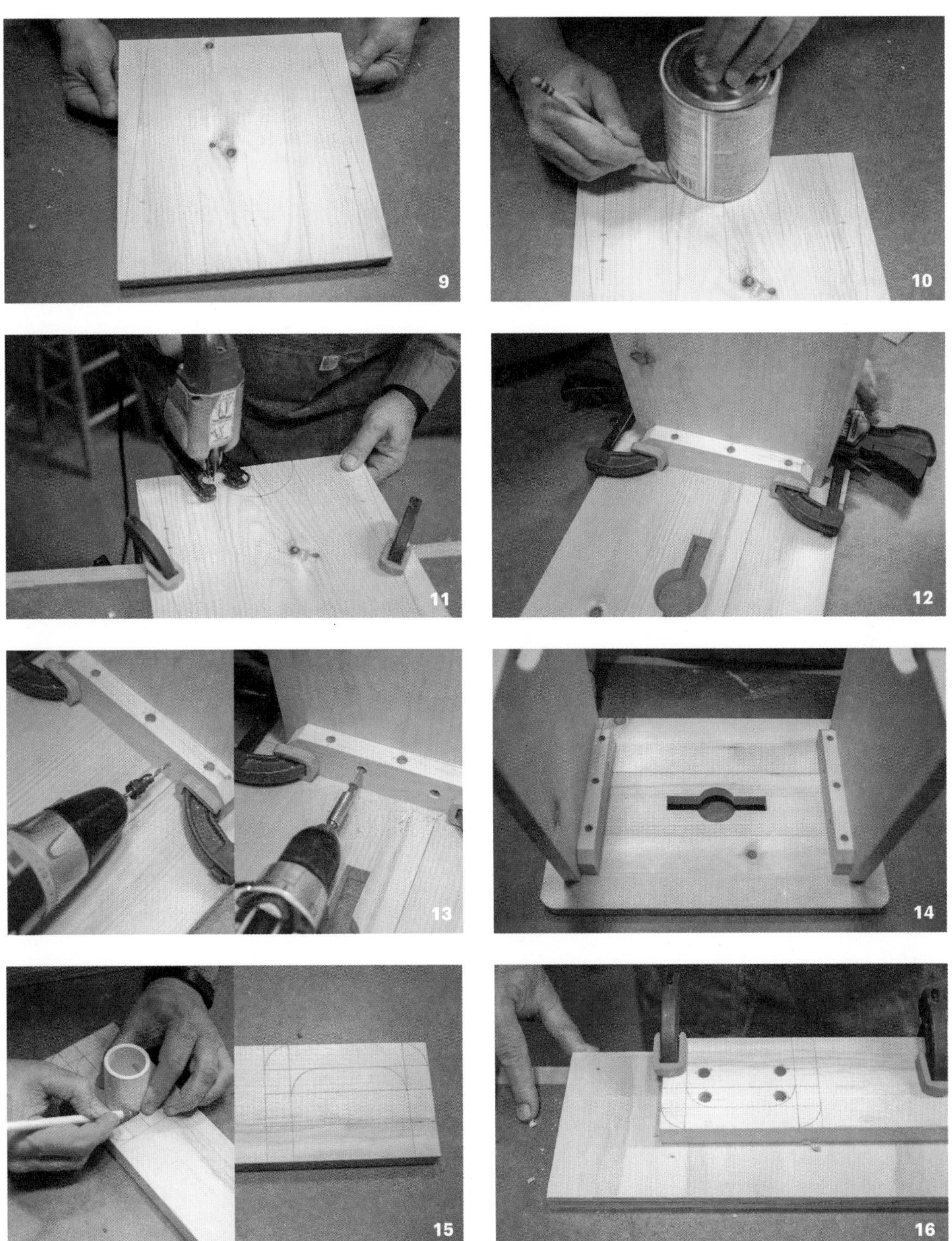
9
10
11
12
13
14
15
16

STEP 7

Installing the Handle

Turn your stool upside down. Cut a piece of Luan plywood measuring ¼" × 2" × 6".

As shown in **figure 22**, attach the plywood with two #8 × ¾" lath screws.

STEP 8

Making the Rails

Select and cut two pieces of pine, each measuring ¾" × 2 ½" × 12 ¼".

Align the pieces to the legs as shown in **diagram D**, then countersink and attach with 1 ¼" deck screws. **(figs. 23–25)**

STEP 9

Making and Installing the Bottom

Cut a piece of Luan plywood measuring ¼" × 9 ½" × 12 ¼".

Attach the plywood to the two rails with four #8 × ¾" lath screws. **(figs. 26–27)**

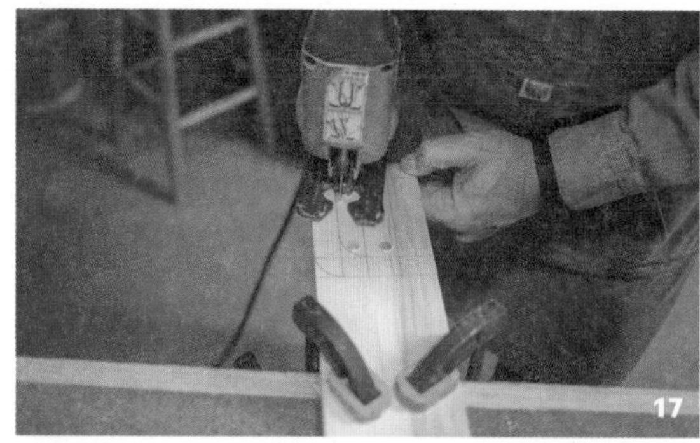
17

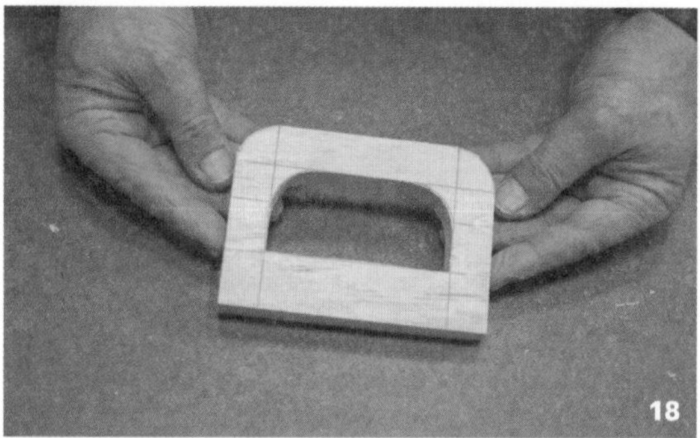
18

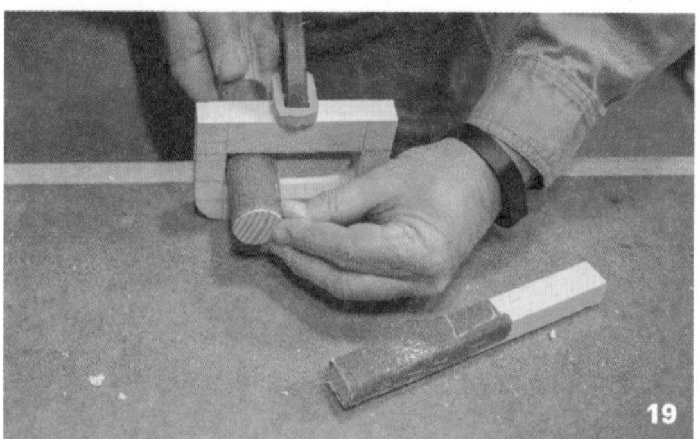
19

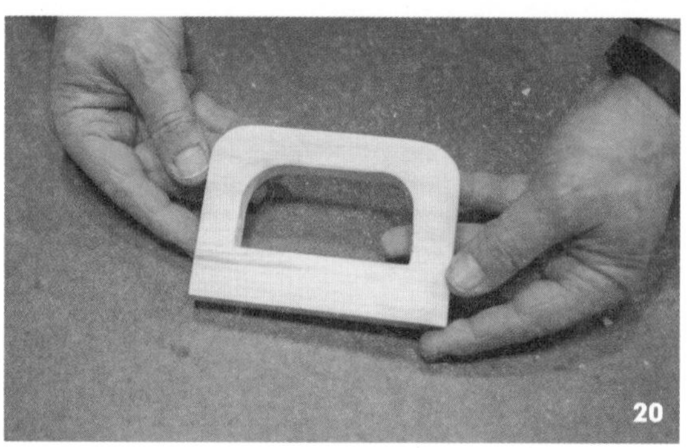
20

21
22
23
24
25
26
27

NOTES

3.

Birdhouse

A birdhouse will add a decorative element to your garden while providing a safe and comfortable place for birds to nest. There is nothing more exciting than seeing birds take up residence in something you have built. During the colder seasons, bird-watching will give you a great way to reconnect with nature, and in most cases you won't even have to leave your home to enjoy it. Start your planning by observing the wild birds that frequent your garden. This will help determine the potential placement of your birdhouse and what size entry hole will work best. With this design, your birdhouse will be well vented and easy to clean, and will weather nicely season after season.

Materials Needed

HARDWARE:

(16) #8 × 1 ½" brass-plated wood screws

(2) 1 ½" brass hinges with screws

TOOLS:

Pencil

Try square

Straight edge

Phillips-head screwdriver

Tape measure

Clamps

Small brush

Waterproof wood glue

Cordless screw gun or corded drill

#6 countersink drill bit

Magnetic tip holder with a #2 Phillips insert bit

⅛" drill bit

1 ¼" Forstner bit

Miter saw or miter box (optional)

Table saw (optional)

Diagram A
Materials & Cutting

A Lid: ¾" × 7 ¼" × 8 ¾"
B Back: ¾" × 6 ½" × 16"
C Front: ¾" × 6 ½" × 10 ½"
D Sides (2): ¾" × 5" × 10 ¾"
E Bottom: ¾" × 5" × 5"

1" × 8" × 96" — Knotted Pine (1 Board)

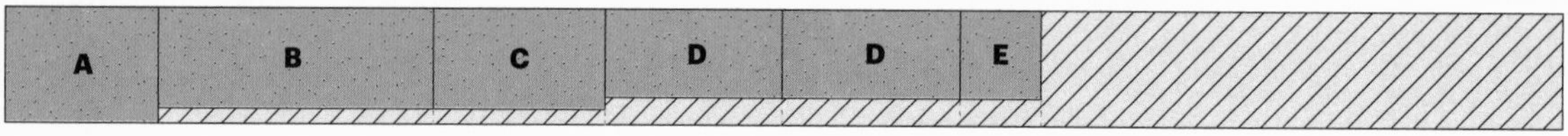

A B C D D E

Diagram B

Diagram C

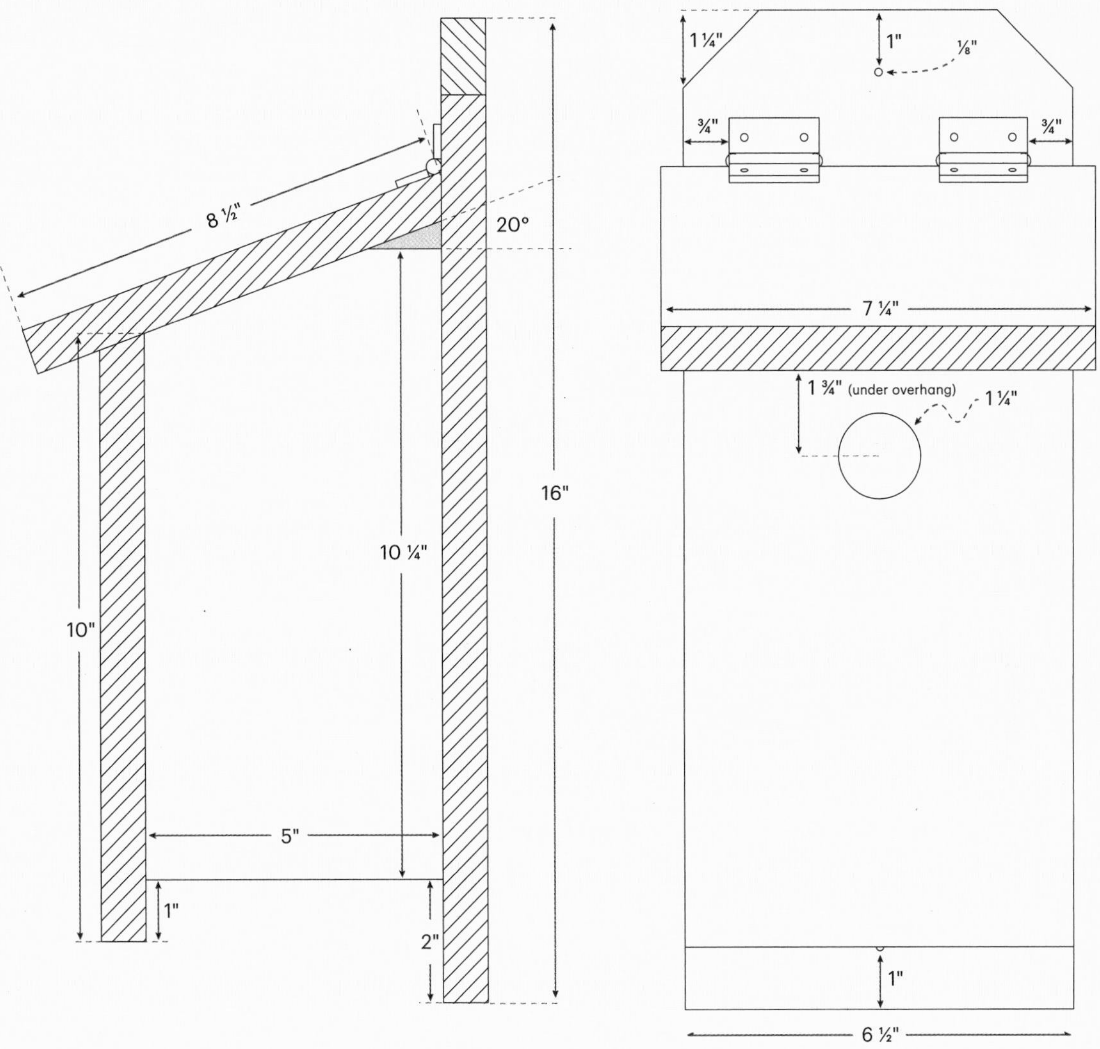

STEP 1

Building the Sides

Select a piece of 1"× 8"× 8' knotted pine. Crosscut it into two 10 ¾" long pieces and rip each piece to 5" wide. Label each piece "side."

> **HELPFUL HINT:** Upon leaving a mill, a 1×8's actual dimensions are ¾" × 7 ¼" as a result of the drying and planing processes.

On both sidepieces, measure and scribe a mark at 1 ¾". Draw an angled line from the mark to the opposite top corner and cut along the line. **(figs. 1–2)**

From the top corners, measure and scribe a line at ½". Use the try square to draw a line from the mark to the angled edge. Then crosscut on the line. **(figs. 3–4)**

STEP 2

Building the Front

Select a piece of 1"× 8" knotted pine. Crosscut one 10 ½" long piece and rip it to 6 ½" wide. Label it "front."

STEP 3

Cutting an Angle on the Frontpiece

Along the top edge, measure in ½" and make a mark. Cut a 20-degree angle on the mark. **(figs. 5–6)**

STEP 4

Cutting the Entry Hole

On the frontpiece, measure and scribe a mark at 3 ¼". Use the try square to draw a line, then measure along the line and mark it at 1 ¾". **(fig. 7)**

Place a piece of scrap wood underneath the frontpiece and clamp them both to your work surface. Using the 1 ¼" Fortsner bit, drill a hole at the mark. **(fig. 8)**

1
2
3
4
5
6
7
8

STEP 5

Attaching the Front to the Sides

As shown in **figure 9**, scribe marks at 1 ¼", 4 ¼", and 7 ¼". Starting at the top, measure along each mark and make a mark in from the edge at ⅜".

Using the small brush, apply waterproof wood glue to the edges of all the pieces. **(fig. 10)**

> **HELPFUL HINT:** Using a clamp is a great way to align and secure your pieces.

Take the #6 countersink bit and drill into the front. Predrill the holes using the ⅛" bit and insert #8 × 1 ½" wood screws with the #2 Phillips bit. **(fig. 11)** Use a damp cloth to remove any excess glue that squeezes out.

STEP 6

Building the Back

Select a piece of 1"× 8" knotted pine. Crosscut one 16" long piece, then rip it to 6 ½" wide and label it "back."

STEP 7

Drilling the Mounting Holes

At each end of the backpiece, measure and scribe a mark at 3 ¼", then draw a line using the try square. Measure along each line and make a mark at 1". **(fig. 12)**

Take the backpiece with a piece of scrap wood underneath it and use the #6 countersink bit to drill the holes. **(figs. 13–14)**

STEP 8

Making the Miter Cuts

At two corners of the backpiece, scribe marks at 1 ¼". Using the straight edge, attach the marks, then cut along the lines. **(fig. 15)**

STEP 9

Making the Overhang Mark

On the backpiece, measure and scribe a mark at 2". Use the try square to draw a line. **(fig. 16)**

STEP 10

Attaching the Back

Starting at the top, measure and mark at 5 ¼", 9 ¼", and 13". Use the try square to draw a line at each mark. Scribe a mark on each line at ⅜". **(fig. 17)**

Apply glue to the back and sidepieces, using the overhang mark to align them. Use a damp cloth to remove any excess glue that squeezes out. **(figs. 18–19)**

Using the #6 countersink bit, drill holes into the back and predrill the holes using the ⅛" bit. Insert #8 × 1 ½" wood screws with the #2 Phillips bit. **(figs. 20–21)**

STEP 11

Building the Lid

Select a piece of 1"× 8" knotted pine. Crosscut one 8 ¾" long piece and label it "lid." On one edge, measure and scribe a mark at ½". Cut a 20-degree angle on the mark. **(figs. 22–23)**

STEP 12

Making and Attaching the Bottom

Select a piece of 1"× 8" knotted pine. Crosscut one 5" long piece and rip it to 5" wide. Apply glue to all the pieces. **(fig. 24)**

Insert the bottom. Use a damp cloth to remove any excess glue that squeezes out. **(fig. 25)**

Measure and scribe marks on the sides at 1 ¼". Scribe along the lines at ⅜" as shown in **figure 26**. Using the #6 countersink bit, drill holes into the bottom, predrilling the holes using a ⅛" bit. Insert #8 × 1 ½" wood screws with the #2 Phillips bit. **(fig. 27)**

STEP 13

Attaching the Lid

Place the lid on the birdhouse and position both hinges ¾" from the edge of the backpiece. Using the ⅛" bit, predrill each hole and insert the screws with the screwdriver.

Adjust the lid and, leaving a ⅜" overhang, predrill and insert the screws. **(fig. 28)**

17
18
19
20
21
22
23
24

25

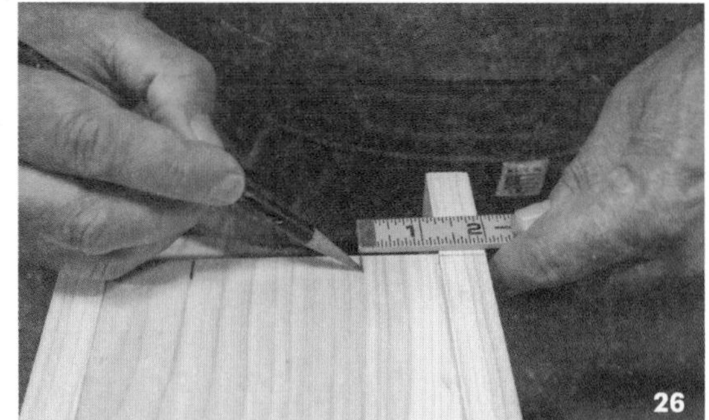
26

27

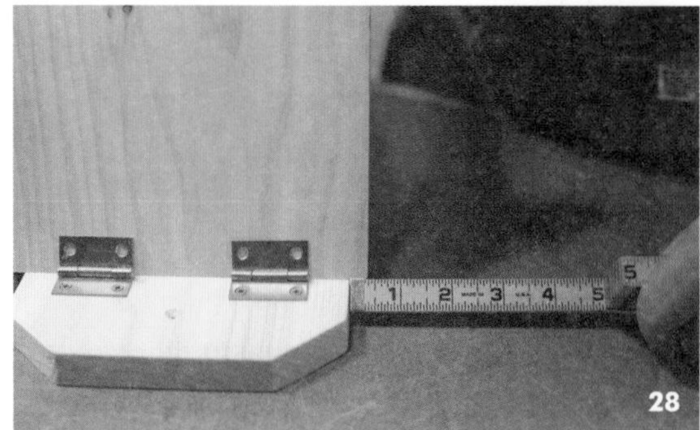
28

NOTES

4.

Birdfeeder

Building a birdfeeder will enable you to study bird behavior and observe different species throughout the changing seasons. This tube feeder can hold an ample amount of seed and is easy to fill and clean. When positioning the feeder in your garden or yard, select an open area that is visible to passing birds; you can hang it on a tree branch or mount it on a post. Birds in flight are especially attracted to this feeder because the seeds appear to be suspended in the air. The natural look of the wood combined with the seeds makes for a comforting sight to every bird.

Materials Needed

HARDWARE:

(9) 1 ⅝" deck screws

(2) #8 × ¾" wood screws

(4) 4' clear tube guard for T12 fluorescent bulbs

(1) ¼" - 20 × 5⁄16" T nut

(1) ¼" - 20 × 1" wing screw

(2) AMP ring terminal 16–14 gauge

(1) 16" vinyl-coated steel wire rope

(1) sheet of 220-grit sandpaper

(1) tube of superglue

(1) ⅛" plastic-coated steel braided cable

TOOLS:

Pencil

Try square

Straight edge

Masking tape

Hammer

Phillips-head screwdriver

Tape measure

Clamps

Utility knife

Crimping pliers

Small brush

Waterproof wood glue

Protective eyewear

Safety gloves

Miter saw or miter box

Cordless screw gun or corded drill

#6 countersink drill bit

Magnetic tip holder with a #2 Phillips insert bit

⅛" drill bit

¼" drill bit

19⁄64" drill bit

1" spade bit

1" Forstner bit

1 ¼" Forstner bit

1 ⅝" Forstner bit

1 ¾" Forstner bit

Radius plane (optional)

Table saw (optional)

Diagram A
Materials & Cutting

A Feed tray: ¾" × 7 ¼" × 7 ¼"
B Lid: ¾" × 7 ¼" × 7 ¼"
C Tube holders (2): ¾" × 7 ¼" × 7 ¼"
D Feed tray rails (4): ¾" × 1 ½" × 8"
Dowel (not shown): 1" Ø × 17 ⅝"

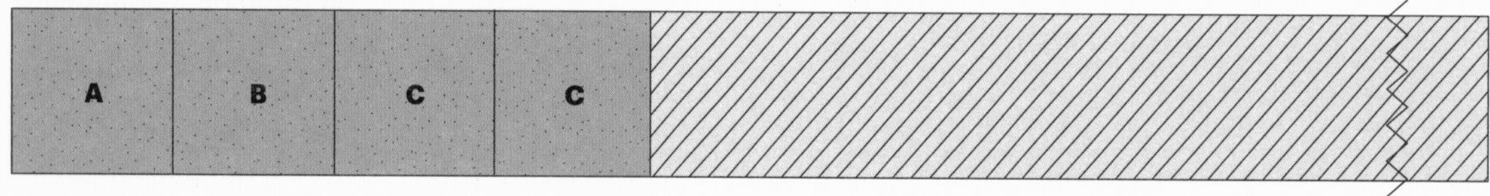

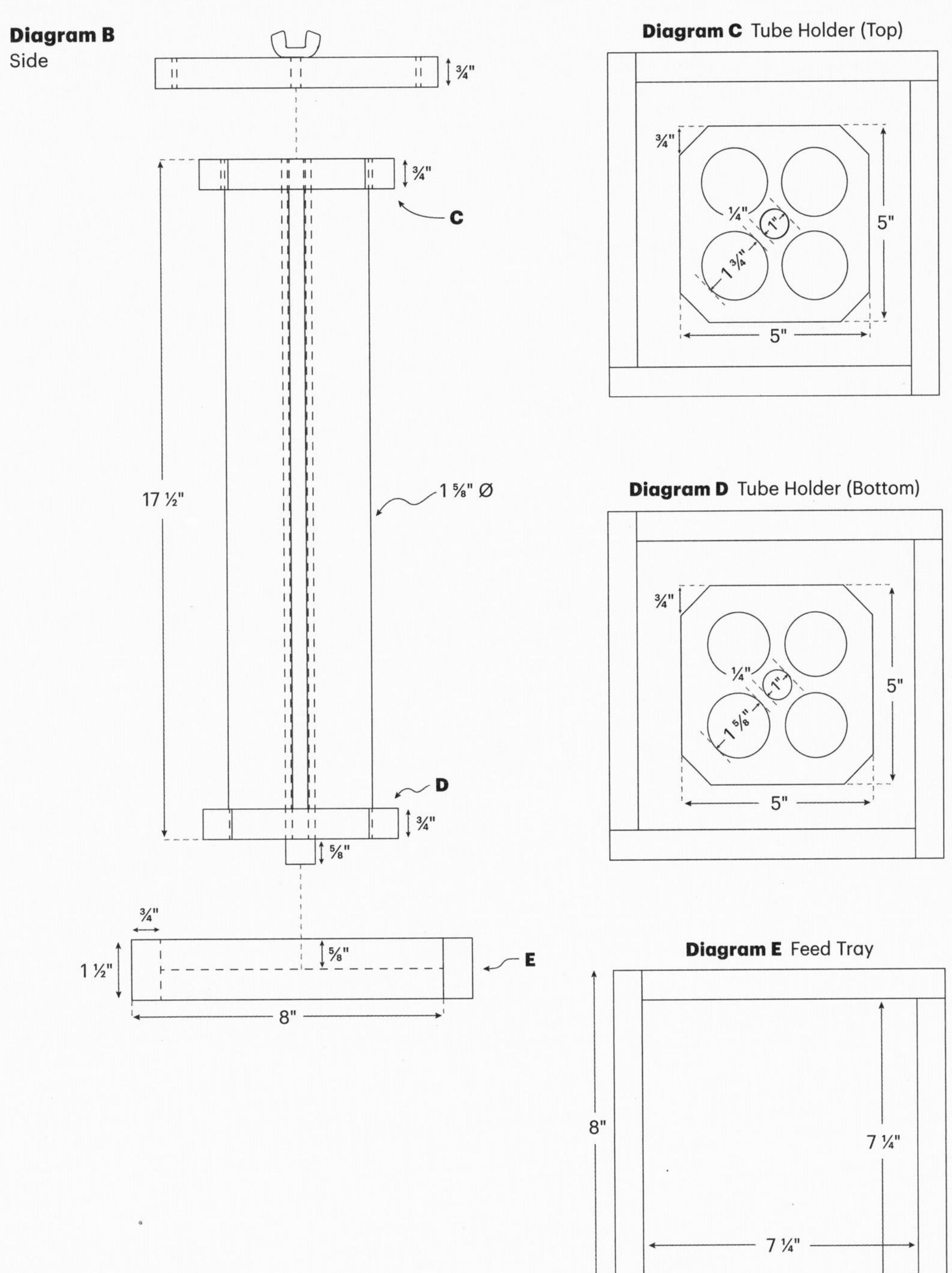
Diagram B
Side
¾"
¾"
C
17 ½"
1 ⅝" Ø
D
¾"
⅝"
¾"
1 ½"
⅝"
E
8"
Diagram C Tube Holder (Top)
¾"
¼"
1"
1 ¾"
5"
5"
Diagram D Tube Holder (Bottom)
¾"
¼"
1"
1 ⅝"
5"
5"
Diagram E Feed Tray
8"
7 ¼"
7 ¼"
8"

STEP 1

Building the Tube Holders

Select a piece of 1" × 8" × 8' knotted pine. Crosscut it into two 7 ¼" long pieces and label one piece "top" and the other "bottom."

HELPFUL HINT: Upon leaving a mill, a 1×8's actual dimensions are ¾" × 7 ¼" as a result of the drying and planing processes.

Using the straight edge, scribe a diagonal line from each corner, locating the center of each board. **(fig. 1)**

STEP 2

Measuring for the Drilling Locations

Take the top and, starting at its center point, measure along each diagonal line, scribing a mark at 1 11⁄16". Do the same on the bottom, scribing a mark at 1 9⁄16". **(fig. 2)**

STEP 3

Drilling the Holes for the Tube Guards and Dowel

Take the top, place a piece of scrap wood underneath, and clamp them both to your work surface. **(fig. 3)**

Fit a drill with the 1 ¾" Forstner bit, align the small tip of the bit on your mark, and drill through the top piece. Repeat to drill on the remaining three marks. **(fig. 4)**

Using the 1" Forstner bit, drill a hole for the dowel through the center point of the top piece.

Repeat the instuctions with the bottom piece, using the 1 ⅝" Forstner bit to drill the holes for the tubes, and the 1" Forstner bit for the dowel. **(fig. 5)**

STEP 4

Trimming the Top and Bottom Pieces

Take both pieces and scribe a mark at 1" on each side. Use the try square to draw a line on each mark. Take the top and bottom pieces and cut along the lines. **(fig. 6)**

1
2
3
4
5
6
7
8

STEP 5

Cutting Off the Corners of the Top and Bottom Pieces

On both the top and bottom pieces, scribe marks ¾" out from each corner. Draw a line connecting each pair of marks and cut along these lines. **(figs. 7–8)**

HELPFUL HINT: After cutting off the corners, keep four of the cutoffs, as they will be helpful later during the glue-up process.

STEP 6

Assembling the Tube Holder

Cut a piece of 1" dowel to 17 ⅝". Using a piece of 220-grit sandpaper, sand the dowel and slightly round one of the ends. **(fig. 9)**

HELPFUL HINT: When inserting the dowel into the top and bottom pieces, there may be a snug fit. Try twisting the dowel like a screw into each hole. You can also use a rubber or wooden mallet to gently tap it in.

Insert the dowel into the bottom piece, leaving a ⅝" overhang. **(fig. 10)**

Insert the dowel into the top piece, making it flush to the very top. Using the straight edge, continue the lines on the top tube holder and across the dowel, locating the dowel's center point. **(fig. 11)**

Place the assembled pieces on a flat surface and make sure they are all aligned correctly. **(fig. 12)**

STEP 7

Making an Assembly Stand

Cut a piece of scrap wood measuring 7 ¼" × 7 ¼". Using the straight edge, draw a diagonal line from each corner, locating the center of the board. Using the 1" spade bit, drill a hole through the board at the center point. **(fig. 13)**

HELPFUL HINT: The assembly stand will help steady your workpiece when gluing and finishing.

STEP 8

Gluing Your Project Together

Take your assembled tube holder and place it in the assembly stand.

Wearing gloves and protective eyewear, apply the superglue to all of the connecting points of the tube holder. Always be sure to glue up in a well-ventilated space. **(fig. 14)**

During the glue-up process, use the corner cutoffs as spacers as shown in **figure 15**.

When you have completed the glue-up process, insert the bottom back into your assembly stand and turn the tube holder upside down. Clamp the two pieces together, then locate the center of the dowel by transferring the intersecting lines on the assembly stand to the dowel. **(fig. 16)**

Using the ⅛" drill bit, drill into the dowel deep enough to accommodate a 1 ⅝" screw. **(fig. 17)**

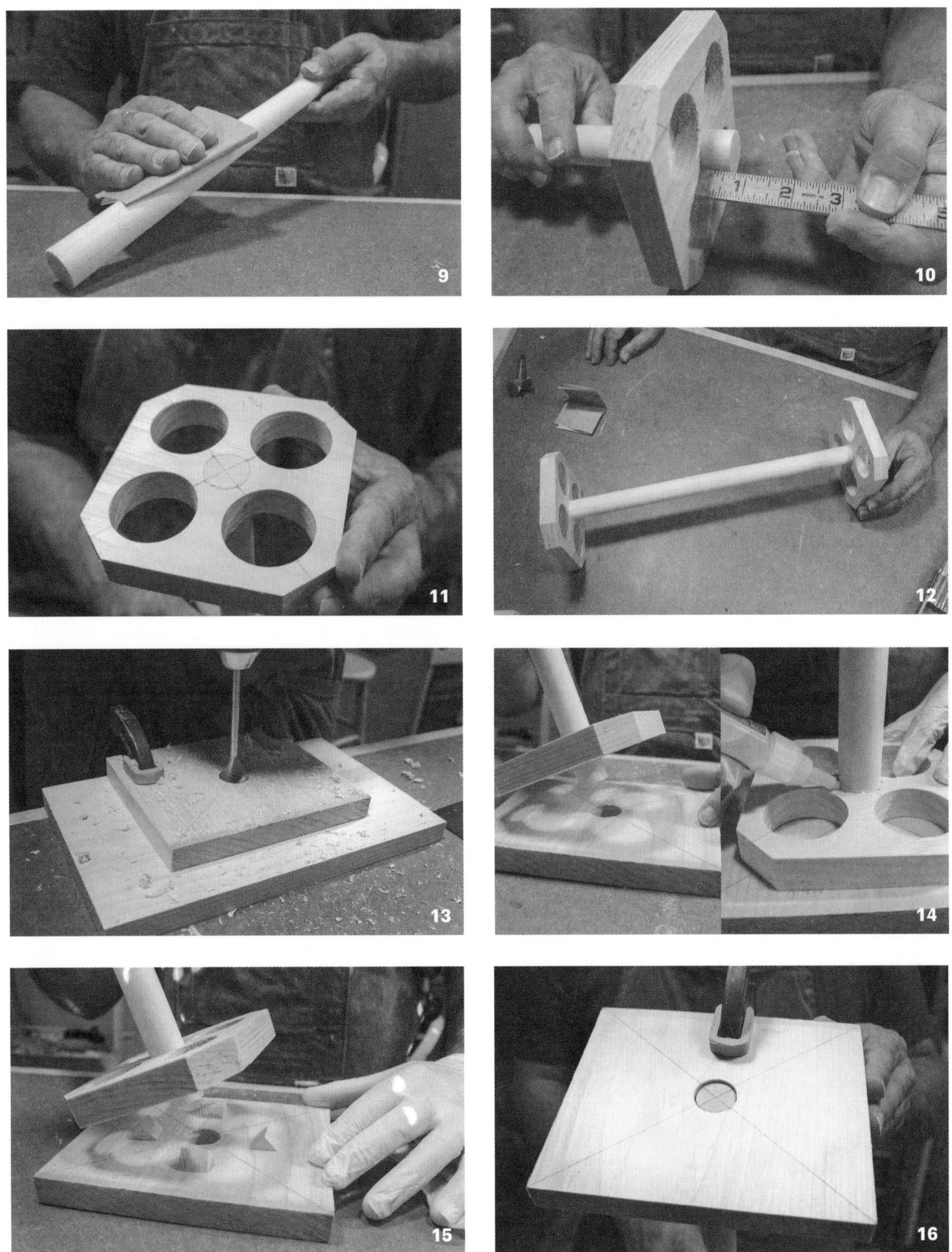
9
10
11
12
13
14
15
16

STEP 9

Inserting a Threaded T Nut

Insert the 5⁄16" bit into a drill. Wrap tape around the tip of the bit at 5⁄8" and drill into the center of the dowel up to the tape as shown in **figure 18**.

Remove all of the sawdust from the hole and apply superglue in and around it. **(fig. 19)**

Use the hammer to gently tap the ¼" - 20 × 5⁄16" T nut into the hole. Once the T nut is seated properly apply more superglue around its edges. **(fig. 20)**

HELPFUL HINT: When applying the superglue, be careful not to get any glue on the T nut threads; superglue can clog the threads and render the T nut useless. Be sure to test the threads by inserting a wing screw.

STEP 10

Building the Feed Tray

Cut a piece of pine measuring ¾" × 7 ¼" × 7 ¼". Using the straight edge, draw a diagonal line from each corner, locating the center of the board. Place a piece of scrap wood under the board. Using the #6 countersink bit, drill a hole through the center point. **(fig. 21)**

Select a piece of pine and crosscut four pieces, each measuring ¾" × 1 ½" × 8". Dry fit them around the perimeter of the feed tray as shown in **figure 22**.

Using the small brush, apply waterproof wood glue to all the pieces. Use a damp cloth to remove any excess glue that squeezes out. **(fig. 23)**

Measure and scribe a mark 1 ½" from each end of the feed tray. Scribe a mark across those lines ⅜" from the bottom of the feed tray. **(fig. 24)**

Using the #6 countersink bit, drill a hole into the sidepieces. Predrill each hole with the ⅛" drill bit. Using the #2 Phillips bit, insert a 1 ⅝" deck screw into each hole. **(fig. 25)**

With all of the sides attached to the feed tray, sand it smooth using 220-grit sandpaper. **(fig. 26)**

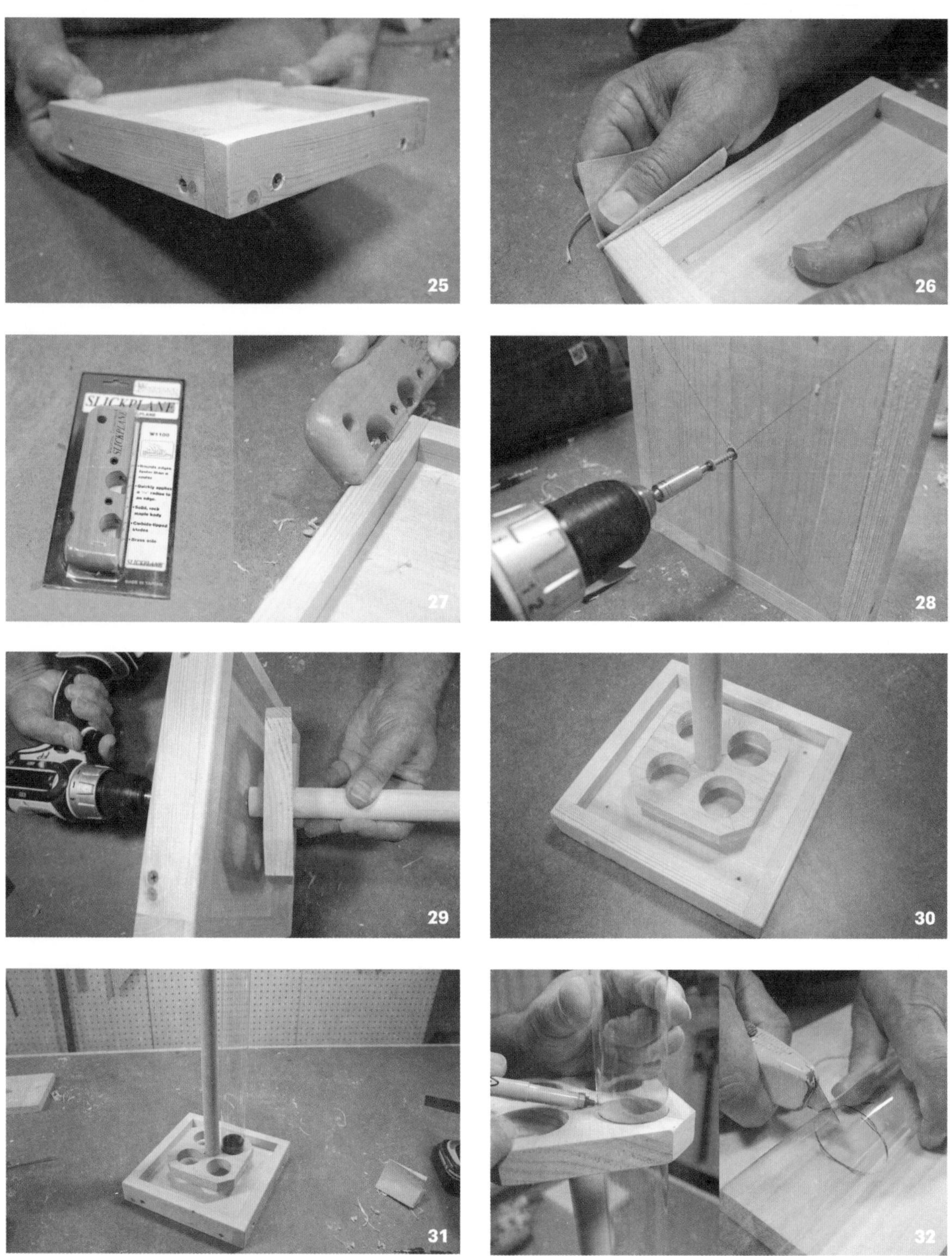
25
26
SLICKPLANE
W1100
27
28
29
30
31
32

HELPFUL HINT: A great tool to use on this project is a radius plane called the "Slickplane." It is priced at around $20 and is manufactured by Woodstock International. It will produce a very nice round-over edge on any project. **(fig. 27)**

STEP 11

Attaching the Feed Tray

Using the #2 Phillips bit, insert one 1 ⅝" deck screw into the hole, letting the tip of the screw protrude slightly out of the feed tray. Align the extended dowel with the tip of the screw. Join the two pieces by tightening the screw. **(figs. 28–29)**

Using the ⅛" bit, drill a weep hole at each corner of the feed tray to allow for water drainage, as shown in **figure 30**.

STEP 12

Sizing the Seed Tubes

Take one of the tube guards and place it in the tube holder. **(fig. 31)**

With a permanent marker, trace a line around the tube guard where it meets the top of the tube holder. Use the utility knife to trim the tube to fit and adjust as needed. **(fig. 32)**

Follow the same sizing and cutting procedures for the remaining tube guards. **(fig. 33)**

HELPFUL HINT: If you find differences in the tube lengths, label each tube to a corresponding hole.

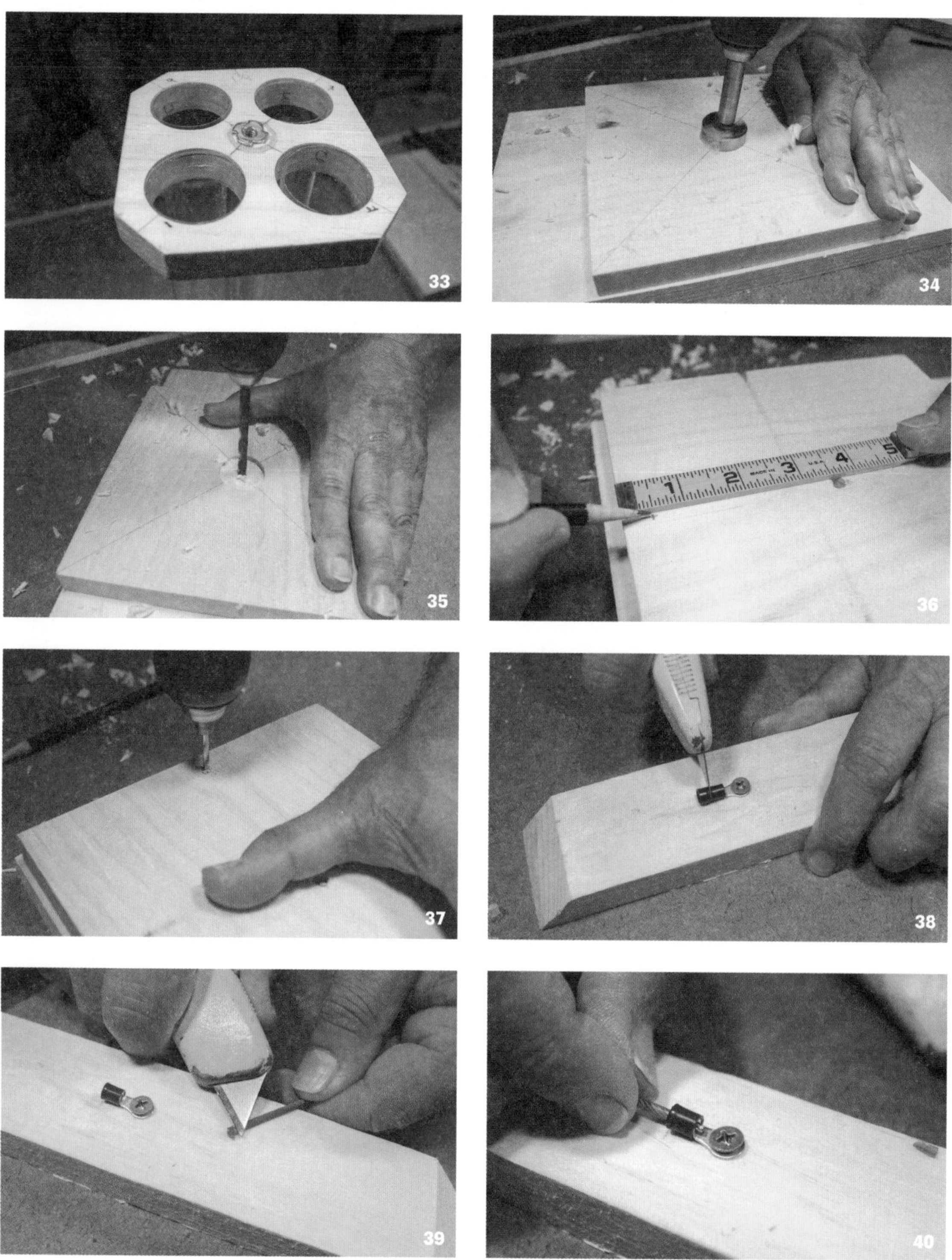
33
34
35
36
37
38
39
40

STEP 13

Making the Lid

Cut a piece of pine measuring ¾" × 7 ¼" × 7 ¼". Using the straight edge, draw a line from each corner locating the center of the board.

Using the 1 ¼" Forstner bit, drill the center of the lid ⅛" deep. Test fit the lid over the T nut, making sure the lid has enough clearance. **(fig. 34)**

Place a piece of scrap wood underneath the lid and, using the ¼" bit, drill a hole through the center of the lid. **(fig. 35)**

On both sides of the lid, measure and scribe a mark at 3 ½", then draw a line along that mark at ½". **(fig. 36)** Using the ⅛" drill bit, drill a hole through the lid. **(fig. 37)**

HELPFUL HINT: If you have a radius plane, use it to round the edges or smooth the edges with 220-grit sandpaper.

Using a #8 × ¾" wood screw, attach the AMP ring terminal to a piece of scrap wood. Then, with the utility knife, cut off half of the plastic portion of the connector. **(fig. 38)**

Take a piece of ⅛" plastic-coated steel braided cable and trim the coating off the ends, making sure it fits into the AMP ring terminal. **(figs. 39–40)**

Using the crimping pliers, squeeze the end of the connector onto the wire. **(fig. 41)** Once the cable is secured to the terminal, take the metal part of the terminal and bend it over 90 degrees. **(fig. 42)**

HELPFUL HINT: You can use regular needle-nose pliers if you don't have crimping pliers on hand.

Thread the cable through the ⅛" holes of the lid and attach another terminal. **(figs. 43–44)**

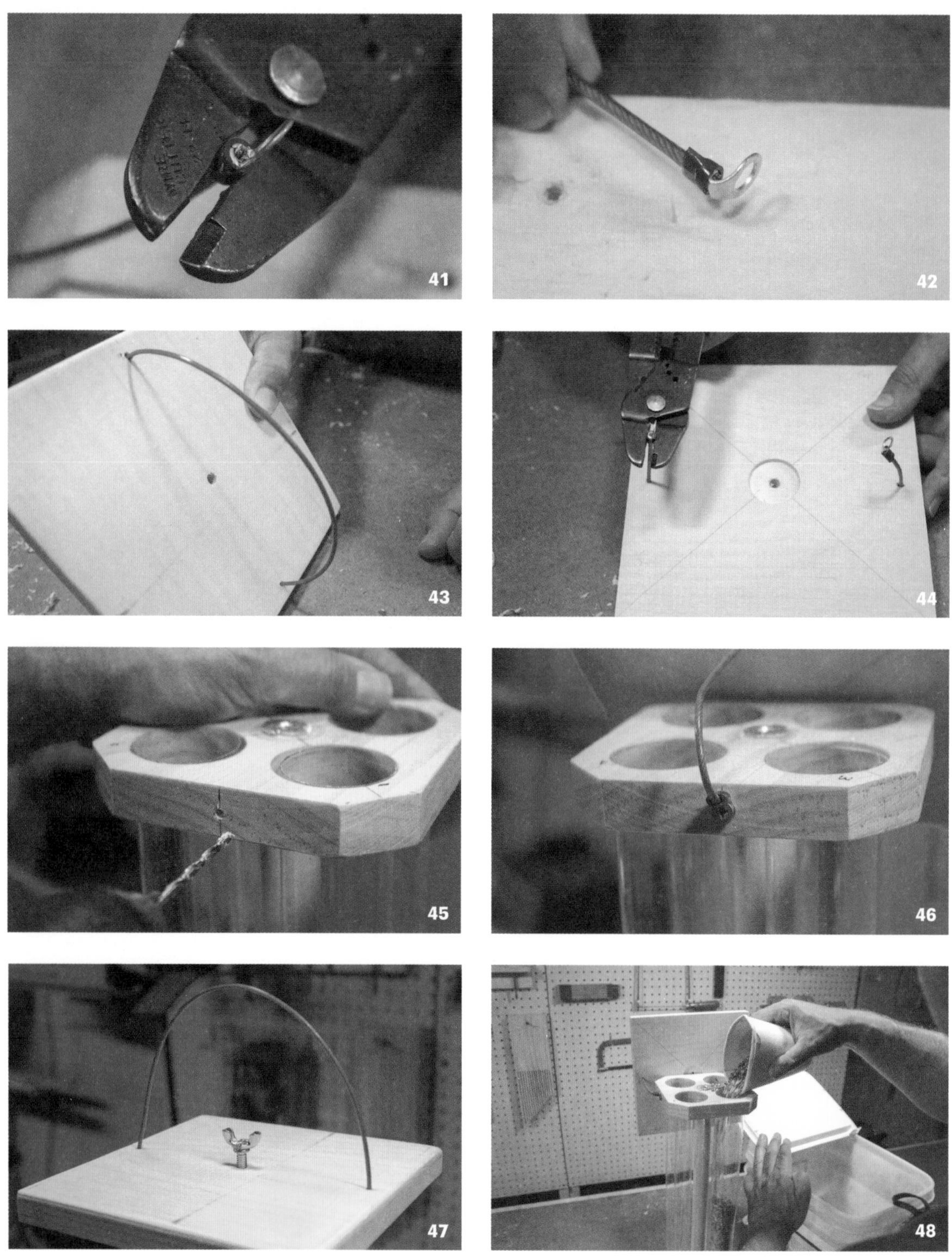
41
42
43
44
45
46
47
48

STEP 14

Attaching the Lid to the Top

Select the two sides that you will attach to the lid to. Measure 1 ¾" and scribe a mark on the top. Use the try square to draw a line across the mark and measure along the line to ⅜". Using the ⅛" bit, drill a ¾" deep hole at the mark. **(fig. 45)**

Using the screwdriver, take a #8 × ¾"screw and attach the ring terminal to the side of the top piece. **(fig. 46)**

Attach the second ring terminal to the opposite side of the top following the same sequence as above.

Attach the lid to the top using a ¼" - 20 × 1" wing screw. **(fig. 47)**

STEP 15

Filling the Birdfeeder

Remove the lid by unscrewing the wing screw, pour the seed into the tubes, and add some seed to the feed tray. **(fig. 48)**

NOTES

5.

Garden Fence

Putting up a fence is a great way to deter unwanted animals from entering or ruining your garden, giving you around-the-clock protection. The type of pest you need to keep out will determine the right fence for you to build. In locations where appearance is important, the design of this fence will allow you to line the base of it with poultry netting (chicken wire) or hardware cloth, preventing animals from digging their way in. Of all the wild animals that may threaten your garden, deer, groundhogs, pocket gophers, rabbits, raccoons, skunks, squirrels, and voles are the most bothersome.

Materials Needed

HARDWARE:

(1) 1 lb. box of 1 ¼" deck screws

(1) 1 lb. box of 1" deck screws

(4) ⅜" electrical cable straps

(2) ½" × 24" rebar

(2) sheets of 220-grit sandpaper

TOOLS:

Pencil

Framing square

Tape measure

Jigsaw or coping saw

Cordless screw gun or corded drill

#6 countersink drill bit

Magnetic tip holder with a #2 Phillips insert bit

⅛" drill bit

Miter saw or miter box (optional)

Table saw (optional)

Diagram A
Materials & Cutting

A Rails (2): ¾" × 2 ½" × 39 ½"
B Pickets (7): ¾" × 2 ½" × 20"
C Jig side: ¾" × 2 ½" × 35"
D Jig side: ¾" × 2 ½" × 23 ¼"
E Jig spacers (12): ¾" × 2 ½" × 2 ½"
F Jig end spacers (4): ¾" × 2 ½" × 3 ¾"
G Jig spacer bars (2): ¾" × 2 ½" × 39 ½"
H Drilling jig: ¾" × 2 ½" × 37"
Pegboard (not shown): ⅛" × 24" × 48"
Drilling jig stops (2) (not shown): ¾" × 1 ¾" × 3"
Jig plywood (not shown): ¼" × 24" × 48"

1" × 3" × 96" — Knotted Pine (5 boards)

Diagram B
Picket Designs

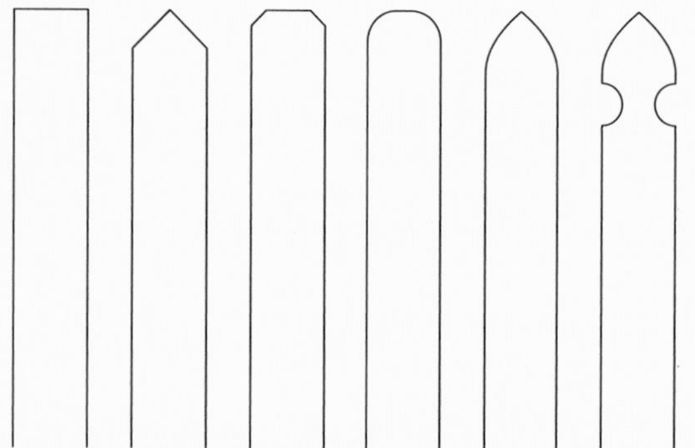

Diagram C
Attaching Multiple Units

additional picket

Diagram D

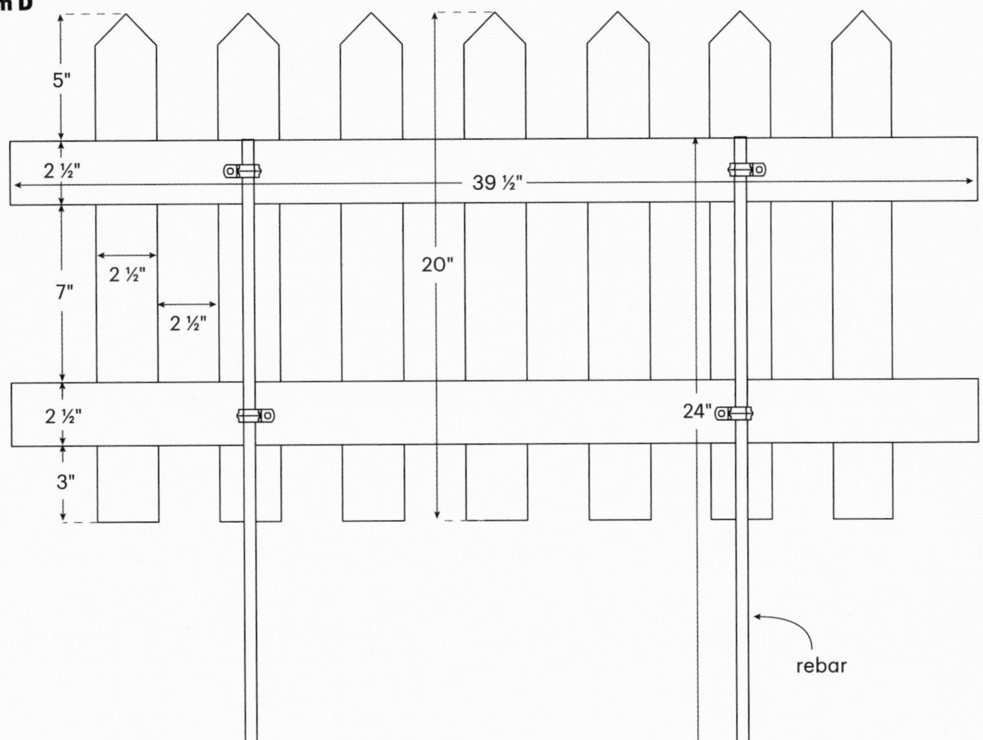

Diagram E

Picket Layout Jig

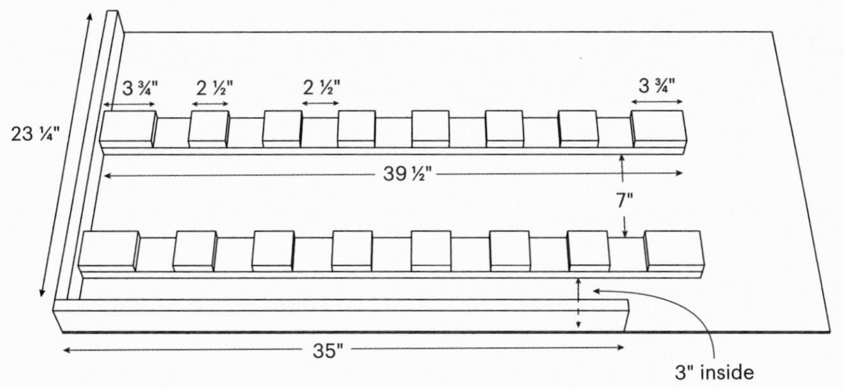

Diagram F

Drilling Jig

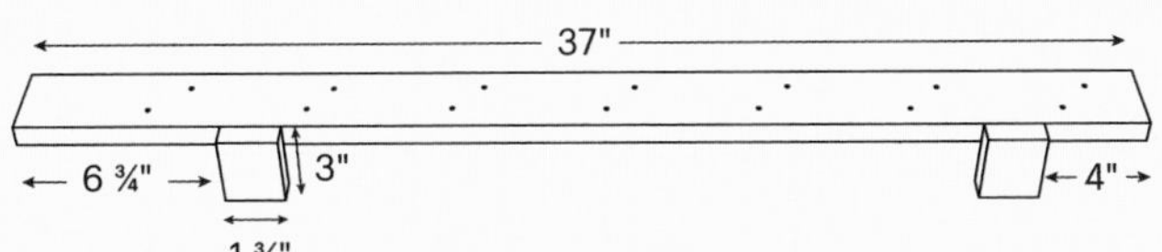

STEP 1

Making the Pickets

Select and cut seven pieces of pine, each measuring ¾" × 2 ½" × 20".

Select the type of picket you would like to make. **(fig. 1)**

STEP 2

Making Spacers for the Layout Jig

See **diagram E** on page 87.

Select and cut two pieces of pine, each measuring ¾" × 2 ½" × 39 ½".

Select and cut twelve pieces of pine, each measuring ¾" × 2 ½" × 2 ½".

Select and cut four pieces of pine, each measuring ¾" × 2 ½" × 3 ¾".

Align one picket in between the spacers as shown in **figure 2**. Attach the spacers by countersinking and screwing with 1 ¼" deck screws. **(figs. 3–4)**

STEP 3

Making the Base for the Layout Jig

Select and cut a piece of Luan plywood measuring ¼" × 24" × 48".

Select and cut two pieces of pine, one measuring ¾" × 2 ½" × 35" and the other measuring ¾" × 2 ½" × 23 ¼".

Using the framing square, align the pieces as shown in **figure 5**.

Once the pieces are squared off, attach the pieces by countersinking and screwing with 1 ¼" deck screws. **(fig. 6)**

Then attach the two pieces to the plywood by countersinking and screwing with 1" deck screws.

STEP 4

Attaching the Spacer Bars

Align the two spacer bars on the plywood. Attach them by countersinking and screwing with 1" deck screws. **(fig. 7)**

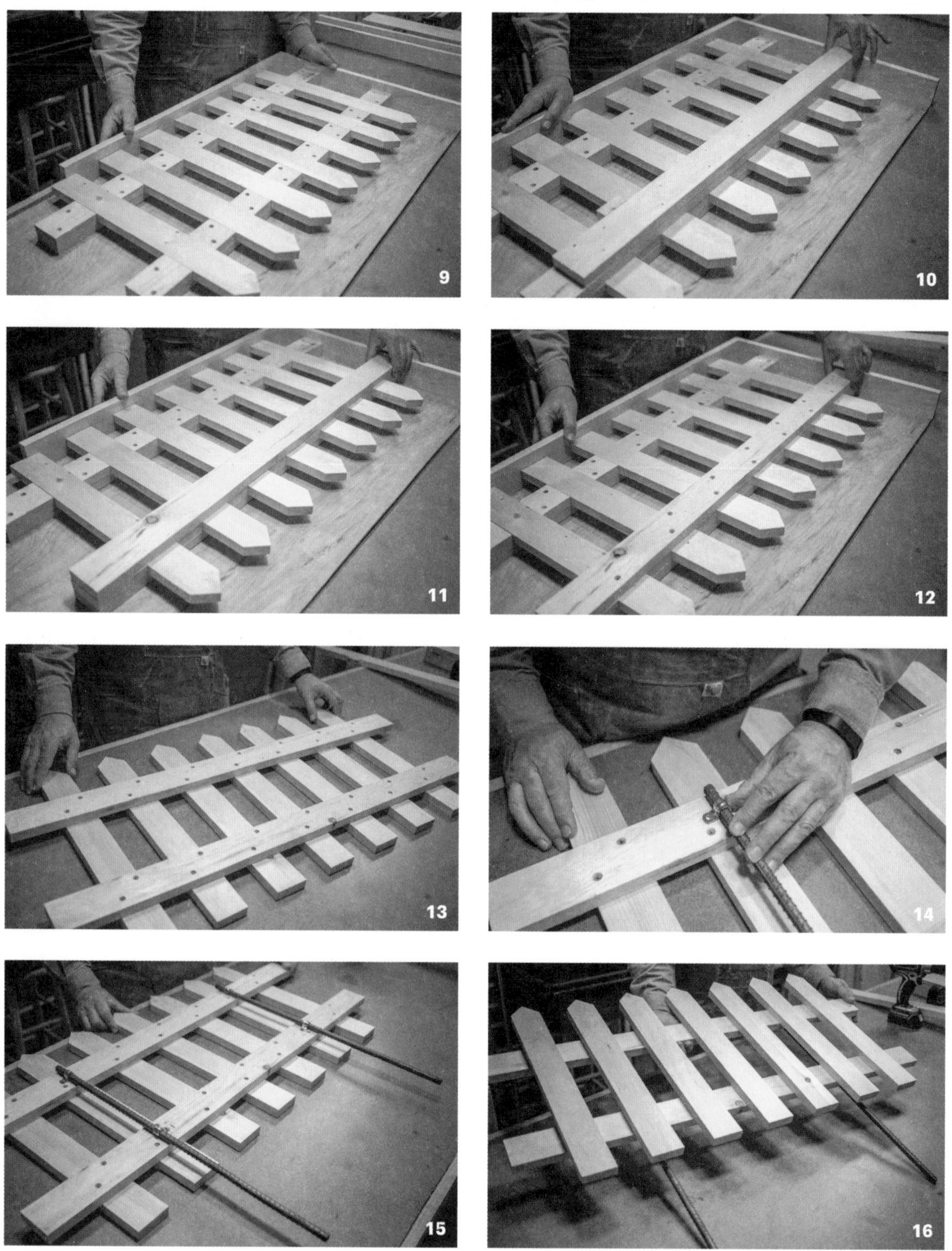
9
10
11
12
13
14
15
16

STEP 5

Making a Drilling Jig

Select and cut a piece of pine measuring ¾" × 2 ½" × 37".

Select and cut two pieces of pine, each measuring ¾" × 1 ¾" × 3".

Attach the two ¾" × 1 ¾" × 3" pieces by countersinking and screwing with 1" deck screws. (See **diagram F** on page 87.)

When using the drilling jig for the fist time, align it on top of the rail. Using the ⅛" bit, drill consecutive holes through the jig. **(fig. 8)**

STEP 6

Making the Rails

Select and cut two pieces of pine, each measuring ¾" × 2 ½" × 39 ½".

STEP 7

Making the Fence

Align the pickets in the layout jig as shown in **figure 9**.

Place a rail onto the pickets. Align the drilling jig on the rail using the ⅛" bit. Predrill the rail. **(figs. 10–11)**

Attach the rail to the pickets by countersinking and screwing with 1 ¼" deck screws. **(fig. 12)**

Repeat the instructions to attach the second rail. **(fig. 13)**

STEP 8

Attaching the Stakes

Position a piece of ½" × 24" rebar onto the rails.

Attach the rebar to the rails using two ⅜" cable straps. Use a 1" deck screw to secure the straps. **(figs. 14–16)**

NOTES

6.

Garden Table

The garden table was designed to be the perfect complement to the garden chair. Together they create a wonderful setting for gatherings, as well as a great place to display plants or your favorite gardening books. Adding this table-and-chair set to your outdoor living space will allow you to sit back and enjoy the beauty of your garden.

HOME HANDBOOKS
GARDEN PLANNING
PERENNIAL
SIMPLY FLOWERS

Materials Needed

HARDWARE:

(1) 1 lb. box of 1 ¼" deck screws

(1) 1 lb. box of 1 ½" deck screws

(1) piece of 1 ½" diameter PVC pipe (2"–3" long)

(2) sheets of 220-grit sandpaper

TOOLS:

Pencil

Try square

Phillips-head screwdriver

Tape measure

Clamps

Jigsaw or coping saw

Cordless screw gun or corded drill

#6 countersink drill bit

Magnetic tip holder with a #2 Phillips insert bit

⅛" drill bit

Miter saw or miter box (optional)

Table saw (optional)

Diagram A
Materials & Cutting

A Slats (10): ¾" × 3 ½" × 24"
B Legs (4): 1" × 2 ¼" × 18 ½"
C Cleats (4): 1" × 2 ¼" × 3 ½"
D Side rails (4): 1" × 2 ¼" × 24"
E Shelf supports (4): 1" × 1 ½" × 19"

1" × 4" × 96" — Knotted Pine (3 boards)

1" × 2 ¼" × 96" — Knotted Pine (3 boards)

1" × 1 ½" × 96" — Knotted Pine (1 board)

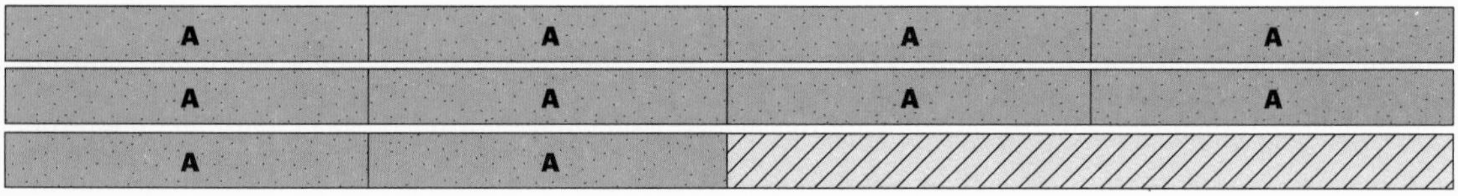

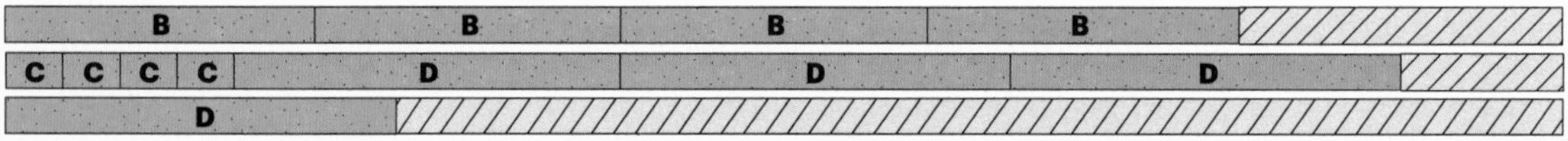

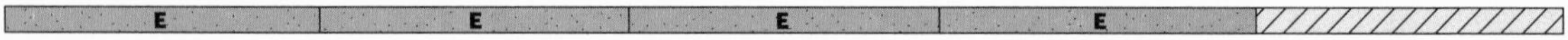

Diagram B
Front

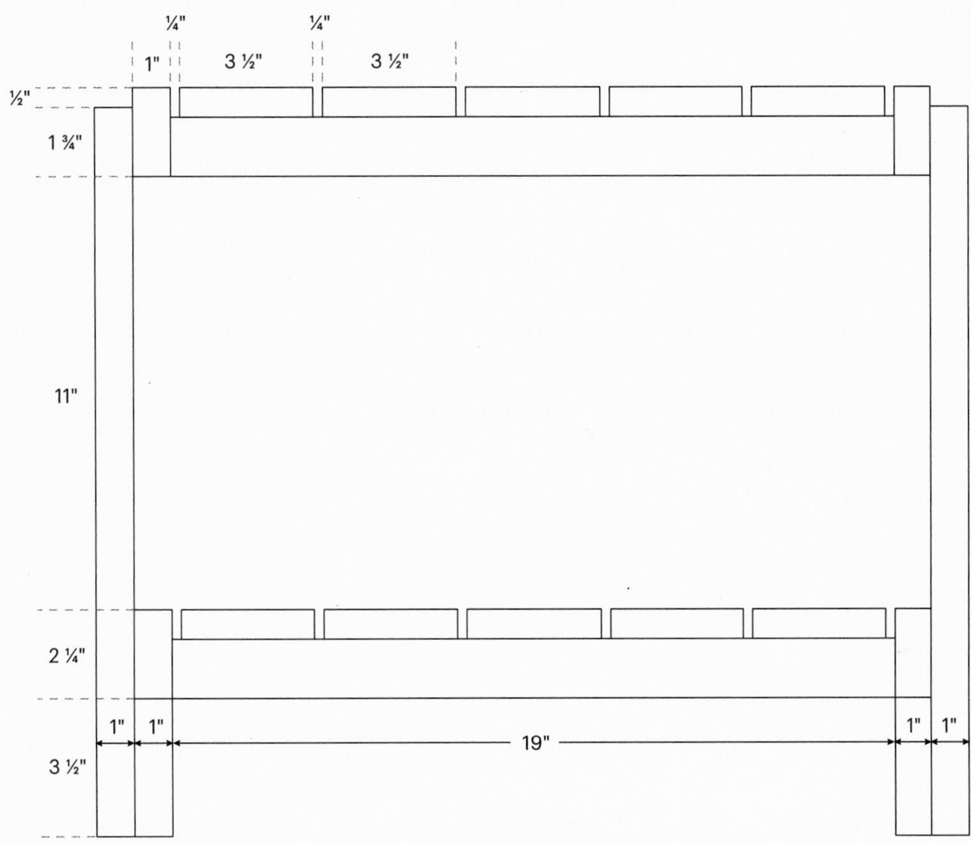

Diagram C
Side

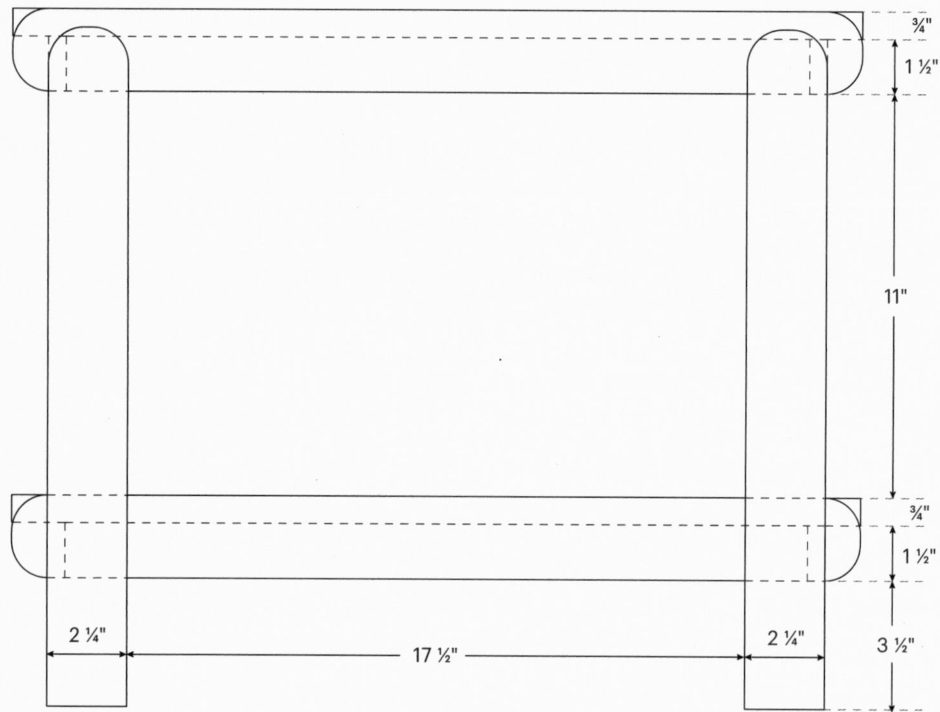

Diagram D
Top

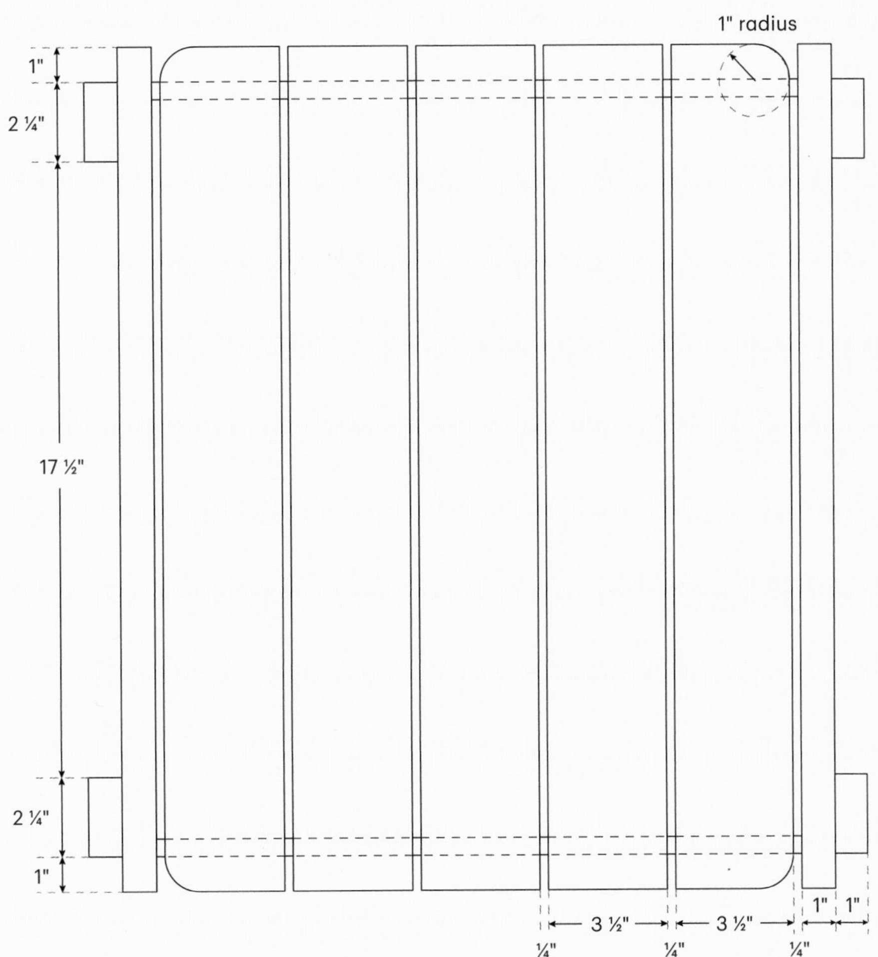

STEP 1

Making the Side Rails

Select and cut two pieces of pine, each measuring 1" × 2 ¼" × 24".

As shown in **figure 1**, use the piece of 1 ½" PVC pipe to create curved corners.

STEP 2

Rounding the Shelf Corners

Using the jigsaw or coping saw, cut along the lines. **(fig. 2)**

HELPFUL HINT: Upon leaving a mill, a 1×8's actual dimensions are ¾" × 7 ¼" as a result of the drying and planing process.

STEP 3

Making the Shelf Supports

Select and cut two pieces of pine, each measuring 1" × 1 ½" × 19".

HELPFUL HINT: Make a jig to create a 1" overhang on each shelf, as shown in **figure 3**.

STEP 4

Making the Frame

Use the try square to help align the pieces. Attach the pieces by predrilling, countersinking, and screwing with 1 ½" deck screws. **(figs. 4–5)**

STEP 5

Making the Slats

Select and cut five pieces of pine, each measuring ¾" × 3 ½" × 24".

STEP 6

Rounding the Slat Corners

Use the piece of PVC pipe to create rounded corners. **(fig. 6)**

HELPFUL HINT: Create a T jig to help you screw the slats to the rails and make connections that are consistent and secure. (**fig. 7**; see page 23)

Lay the slats out on a level work surface, positioning the frame on top of the slats, then place ¼" spacers in between the slats.

HELPFUL HINT: Use a clamp to secure a piece of wood to your work surface. This will keep the slat and frame pieces aligned while you attach them. **(fig. 8)**

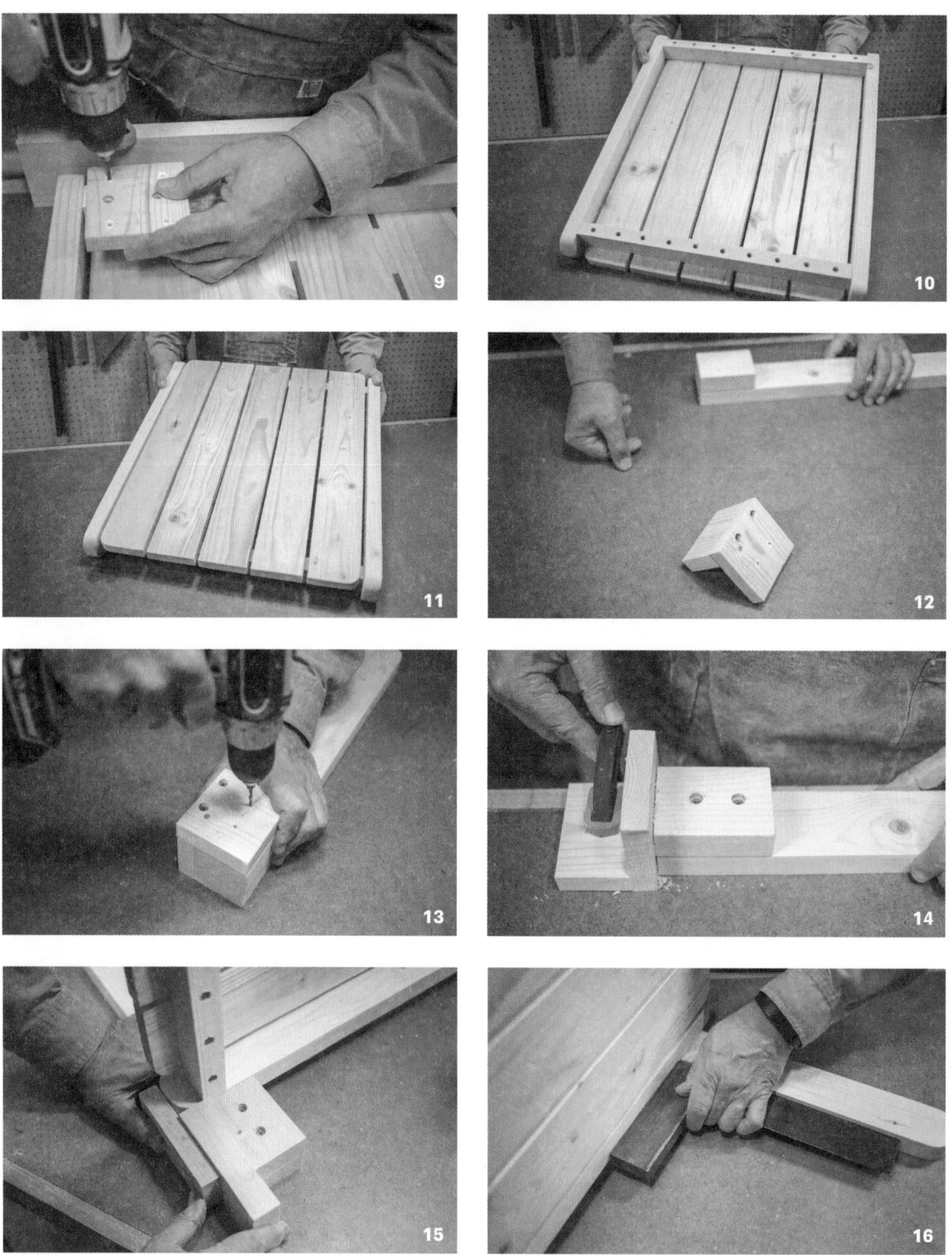
9
10
11
12
13
14
15
16

STEP 7

Attaching the Slats

Using a jig, predrill each hole with the ⅛" bit, then countersink and attach with two 1 ½" deck screws. **(figs. 9–11)**

STEP 8

Making the Legs

Select and cut four pieces of pine, each measuring 1" × 2 ¼" × 18 ½". Use the piece of PVC pipe to create curved corners at the top of each leg.

STEP 9

Attaching Cleats to the Legs

Select and cut four pieces of pine, each measuring 1" × 2 ¼" × 3 ½".

HELPFUL HINT: Create a jig to help create consistent and secure connections when attaching the pieces together. **(fig. 12)**

Using a jig, predrill each hole with the ⅛" bit, then countersink and attach with two 1 ½" deck screws. **(fig. 13)**

As shown in **figure 14**, use the jig to align the pieces when attaching the cleat to the leg.

STEP 10

Attaching the Legs

As shown in **figure 15**, use a jig to leave a 1" overhang at the leading edge of each shelf.

Using the try square, align your legs to the shelf. **(fig. 16)**

Attach the legs by countersinking two staggered holes. Screw the pieces together with two 1 ½" deck screws at each connecting point. **(fig. 17)**

When you're done attaching the legs, stand the table on a level surface and adjust as needed. **(fig.18)**

STEP 11

Attaching the Top Shelf

As shown in **figure 19**, use a jig as a guide to leave a 1" overhang at the leading edge of the shelf. Cut a piece of scrap wood measuring 11" long. This piece will help to keep the distance between the two shelves.

Attach the legs by countersinking two staggered holes. Screw the pieces together with two 1 ½" deck screws. **(fig. 20)**

17

18

19

20

NOTES

7.

Compost Bin

If you're looking for a resourceful way to add nutrients to your garden, you can produce your own fertilizer in a compost bin. The ingredients needed to create rich compost are separated into three types. The first is dry materials, which consist of dead leaves, branches, and twigs; the second is green materials, made up of grass clippings and vegetable and fruit waste; and the last is water. When selecting a location for your compost bin, make sure it's close to a water source, and in a shaded area. Always load your materials by type, adding water in between each layer. By just overturning the bin a few times, you can easily mix its contents. Composting is a natural and economical method for replenishing your garden's soil, and will reduce your need for chemical fertilizers.

Materials Needed

HARDWARE:

(1) 1 lb. box of 1 ¼" deck screws

(3) #8 × 1" brass-plated wood screws

(1) 1 ½" galvanized barrel bolt with galvanized screws

(2) yards of fiberglass screening

(1) box of ¼" staples

TOOLS:

Pencil

Try square

Framing square

Phillips-head screwdriver

Tape measure

Staple gun

Spring clamps

Cordless screw gun or corded drill

#6 countersink drill bit

Magnetic tip holder with a #2 Phillips insert bit

⅛" drill bit

5/16" drill bit

Miter saw or miter box (optional)

Table saw (optional)

Diagram A
Materials & Cutting

A Legs (4): ¾" × 3 ½" × 27 ¾"
B Sides (10): ¾" × 3 ½" × 23 ¾"
C Front (5): ¾" × 3 ½" × 23 ¾"
D Back (5): ¾" × 3 ½" × 23 ¾"
E Lid (5): ¾" × 3 ½" × 20 ¾"
F Bottom (5): ¾" × 3 ½" × 20 ¾"
G Side horizontal cleats (4): ¾" × ¾" × 20 ¾"
H Side vertical cleats (4): ¾" × ¾" × 19 ¼"
I Front cleats (4): ¾" × ¾" × 17 ⅜"
J Back cleats (4): ¾" × ¾" × 17 ⅜"
K Lid cleats (2): ¾" × ¾" × 16 ¾"
Dowel (not shown): ½" Ø × 19"

1" × 4" × 96" — Knotted Pine (9 boards)

A A A
A B B
B B B B
B B B B
C C C C
C D D D
D E E E
E E F F
F F F D

1" × 1" × 96" — Knotted Pine (4 boards)

G G G G
H H H H
I I I I K
J J J J K

Diagram B
Front / Back

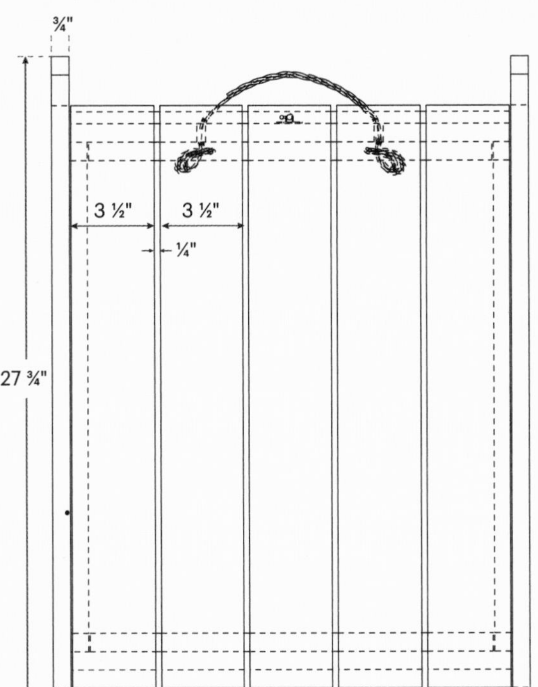

Diagram C
Side

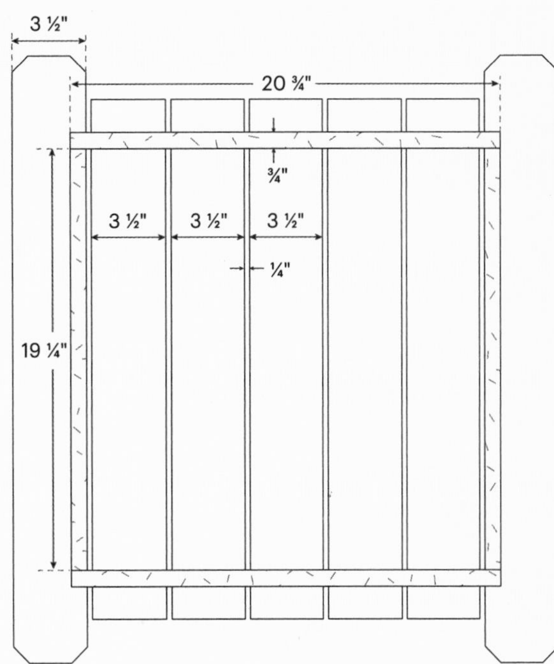

Diagram D
Assembling the Side

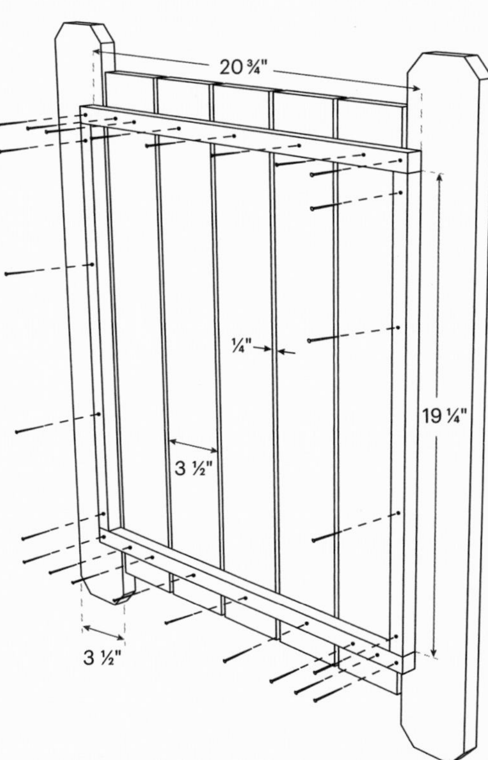

STEP 1

Making the Sides and Legs

Select and cut seven pieces of pine, five measuring ¾" × 3 ½" × 23 ¾" and two measuring ¾" × 3 ½" × 27 ¾".

As shown in **figure 1**, lay the pieces out on your work surface, then place ¼" spacers in between them.

> **HELPFUL HINT:** Use a piece of scrap wood to help align the pieces to the front edge of your work surface.

Position the two legs on your work surface using a 2" measuring block to determine the overhang of the legs. **(fig. 2)**

Measure in ¾" from each corner of the leg and cut a 45-degree angle. (**fig. 3**; see **diagram C** on page 107)

Select and cut four pieces of pine, two measuring ¾" × ¾" × 20 ¾" and two measuring ¾" × ¾" × 19 ¼".

Position these pieces to create a frame as shown in **figure 4**.

> **HELPFUL HINT:** Create measuring blocks to help with the alignment of the frame pieces.

Create a jig to help mark where to attach the frame pieces. **(fig. 5)**

Using the try square, transfer the marks from the jig to the frame pieces. Attach the pieces by predrilling with the ⅛" bit, countersinking, and screwing with 1 ¼" deck screws. **(fig. 6)**

Repeat the instructions to make the remaining side and leg.

STEP 2

Making the Front and Back

Select and cut five pieces of pine, each measuring ¾" × 3 ½" × 23 ¾".

Lay the pieces out on your work surface, then place ¼" spacers in between the pieces.

Select and cut two pieces of pine, each measuring ¾" × ¾" × 17 ⅜".

With the measuring blocks, align the frame pieces as shown in **figure 7**.

Using the try square and the marking jig, transfer the screw locations. Attach the pieces by predrilling with the ⅛" bit, countersinking, and screwing with 1 ¼" deck screws. **(fig. 8)**

Repeat the instructions to make the back section.

STEP 3

Making the Lid and Lid Cleats

Select and cut five pieces of pine, each measuring ¾" × 3 ½" × 20 ¾".

Lay the pieces out on your work surface, then place ¼" spacers in between each piece.

Select and cut two pieces of pine, each measuring ¾" × ¾" × 16 ¾". Position the two pieces on the lid slats.

Using the try square and the marking jig, transfer the screw locations. Attach the pieces by predrilling with the ⅛" bit, countersinking, and screwing with 1 ¼" deck screws. **(fig. 9)**

STEP 4

Attaching the Handle

Find the locations for the two evenly spaced holes needed for the handle. Using the ⅜" bit, drill two holes through the lid. **(fig. 10)**

HELPFUL HINT: To prevent tear-out on the exit hole when drilling, place a piece of scrap wood underneath the piece you're working on.

Use a small Phillips-head screwdriver to push the ¼" braided rope through the holes.
Fit the rope through the holes and tie the ends with overhand knots, as shown in **figures 11–12.**

STEP 5

Assembling the Bin

Place the frontpiece and a sidepiece on your work surface.

Using the framing square and spring clamps, align the two pieces. **(fig. 13)**

HELPFUL HINT: Predrill all of the connection locations prior to assembly. **(fig. 14)**

Connect the two pieces by predrilling with the ⅛" bit, countersinking, and screwing with 1 ¼" deck screws.

HELPFUL HINT: As shown in **figure 15**, use quarters as spacers during assembly process. The space created by the quarters will give the lid a looser fit and compensate for the wood expanding and contracting during different seasons.

Repeat the instructions to make the remaining sidepiece and the backpiece. **(fig. 16)**

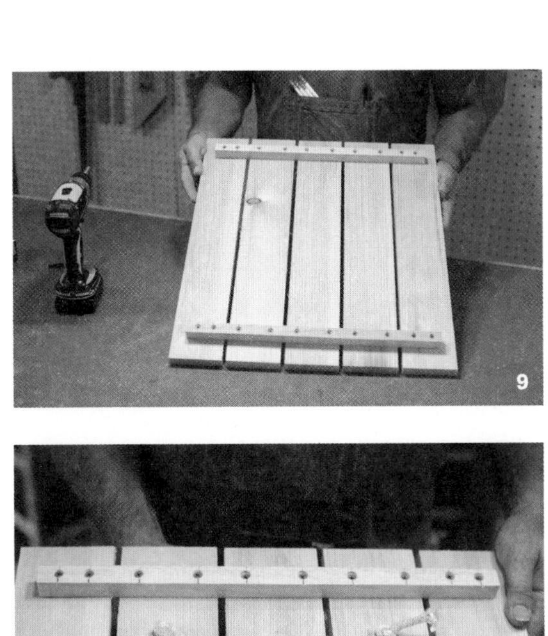
9

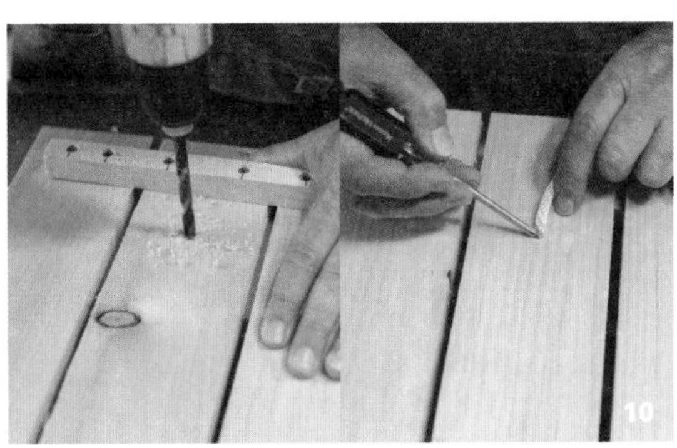
10

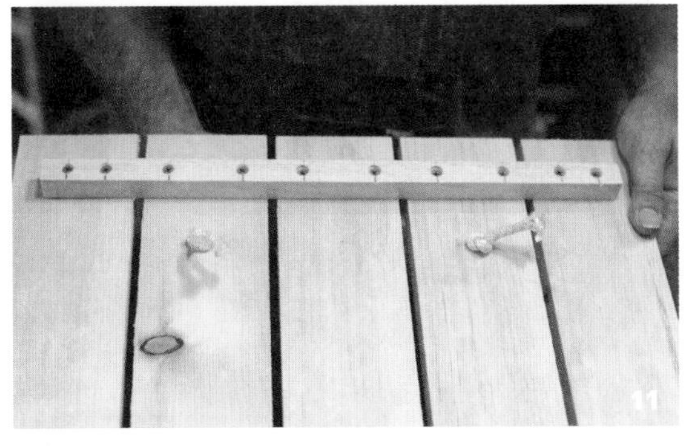
11

12

13

14

15

16

STEP 6

Attaching the Bottom

Place the compost bin upright on a level floor. As shown in **figure 17**, use the framing square to square off the bin.

Select and cut five pieces of pine, each measuring ¾" × 3 ½" × 20 ¾".

Test fit the five pieces in the bottom of the bin. **(fig. 18)**

HELPFUL HINT: Create a hole-making jig to prep the bottom pieces as shown in **figures 19 and 20**.

Attach the bottom pieces by predrilling with the ⅛" bit, countersinking, and screwing with 1 ¼" deck screws. **(fig. 21)**

STEP 7

Installing the Screen

HELPFUL HINT: The screen is used to hold the small particulates in the bin when the composting process is at its last stages.

Attach the screening material using the staple gun with ¼" staples. **(fig. 22)**

HELPFUL HINT: There is really no science to this procedure. The screening material should be overlapped and the stapling can be done in random patterns. **(fig. 23)**

Start by lining the bottom section of the bin. Extend the bottom pieces up along the sides by 2" to 3". Overlap the sidepieces, trimming them at the bin's top edge.

STEP 8

Installing the Dowel Rod

Select and cut a piece of dowel measuring ½" × 19".

With the lid in place, fit the dowel in between the two sidepieces. Use two quarters as spacers underneath the dowel. **(fig. 24)**

As shown in **figure 25**, measure and scribe marks for each screw location.

HELPFUL HINT: On your work surface, predrill the dowel with a countersink bit. Using a piece of scrap wood underneath the dowel will help to prevent tear out of the exit hole. **(fig. 26)**

Attach the dowel to the bin with three #8 × 1" brass-plated wood screws. **(fig. 27)**

17
18
19
20
21
22
23
24

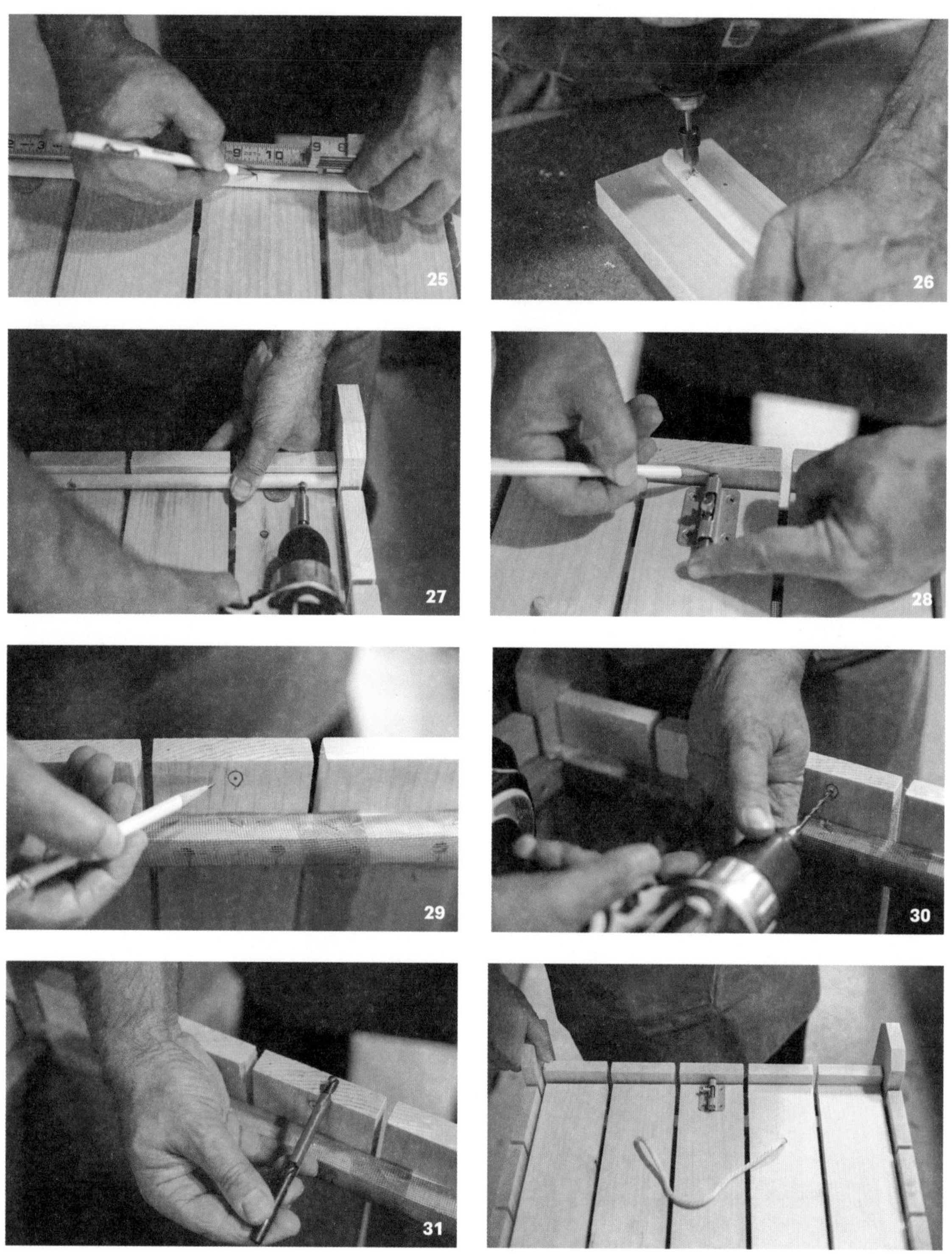
25
26
27
28
29
30
31

STEP 9

Attaching the Barrel Bolt

As shown in **figure 28**, locate the correct position of the 2 ½" galvanized barrel bolt on the bin's lid. Scribe marks for the screws' locations.

> **HELPFUL HINT:** To prevent the wood from splitting, predrill each screw hole with the ⅛" bit.

Using the Phillips-head screwdriver, fasten the barrel bolt to the lid. Once the barrel bolt is attached, scribe a mark where the bolt makes contact with the bin.

Locating the center of this mark, predrill the hole with the ⅛" bit. **(figs. 29–30)**

> **HELPFUL HINT:** Predrilling a hole with a smaller bit will help to guide the path of a larger bit.

Use a piece of tape to mark the desired drilling depth. In this case, use a 5⁄16" bit and drill a ½" deep hole. **(fig. 31)**

NOTES

8.

Fan Trellis

Fan-style trellises provide an elegant and simple way to dress up and add a broad range of colors and fragrances to your garden. By selecting and growing climbing flowers, foliage, or berries, you can transform any bare wall. Going vertical will allow you to expand a small vegetable garden or create a decorative privacy screen around a sitting area.

Materials Needed

HARDWARE:

(1) 1 lb. box of 1 ¼" deck screws

(2) sheets of 220-grit sandpaper

TOOLS:

Pencil

Try square

Phillips-head screwdriver

Waterproof wood glue

Small brush

Tape measure

Clamps

Jigsaw or coping saw

Cordless screw gun or corded drill

#6 countersink drill bit

Magnetic tip holder with a #2 Phillips insert bit

⅛" drill bit

1" spade bit

Miter saw or miter box (optional)

Table saw (optional)

Diagram A

Materials & Cutting

1" × 6" × 96" — Knotted Pine

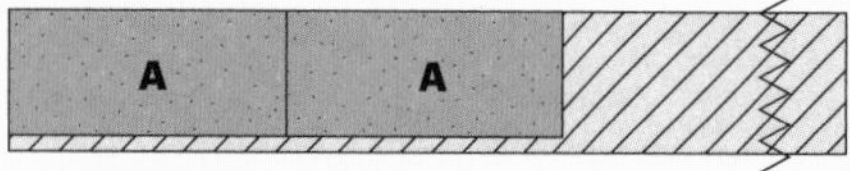

A Base, front and back: ¾" × 5 ½" × 12"

B Base, sides: ¾" × ⅞" × 12"

C Top brace: ¾" × 2" × 44"

D Middle brace: ¾" × 2" × 17"

E Vertical pieces (7): ½" × ¾" × 84"

Base plug (not shown): ¾" × ⅞" × 3"

1" × 2" × 96" — Knotted Pine

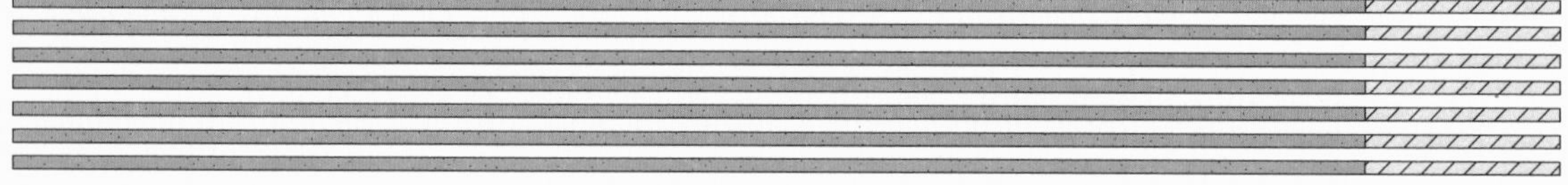

E ½" × ¾" × 96" — Knotted Pine (7 boards)

Diagram B

Holes

Upper Brace

44"

2"

Center line

1 ½"

Spaced 7" apart

1" diameter holes on center

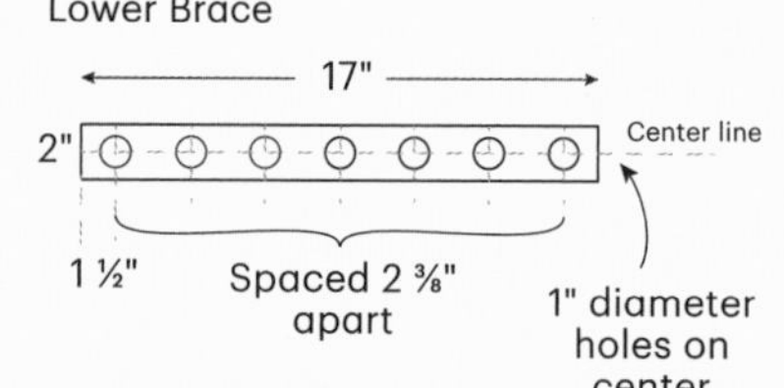

Diagram C

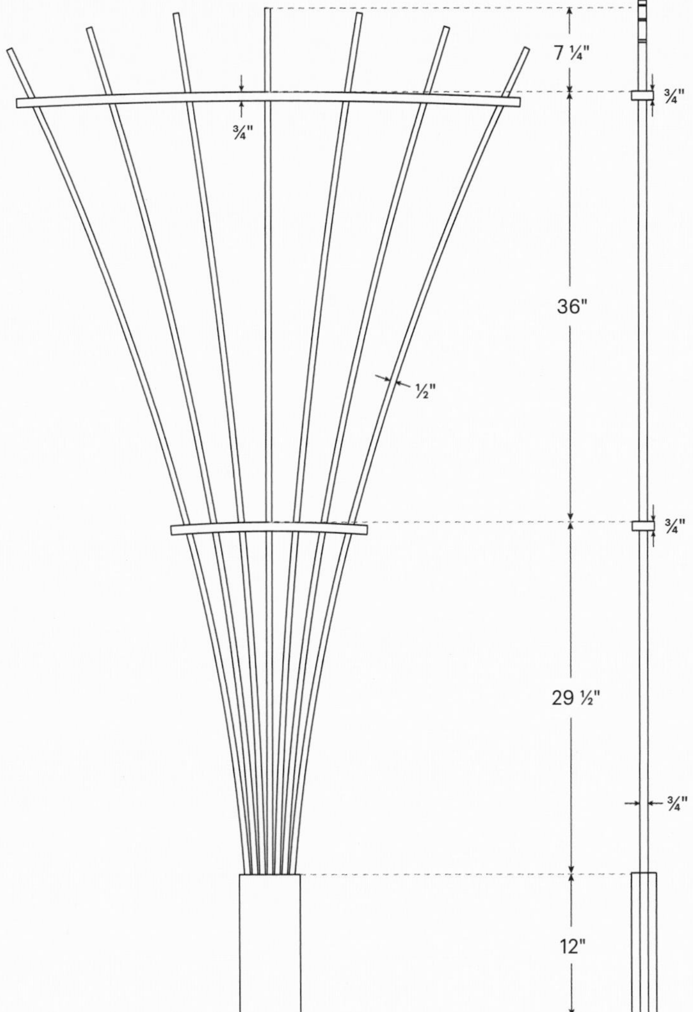

Diagram D

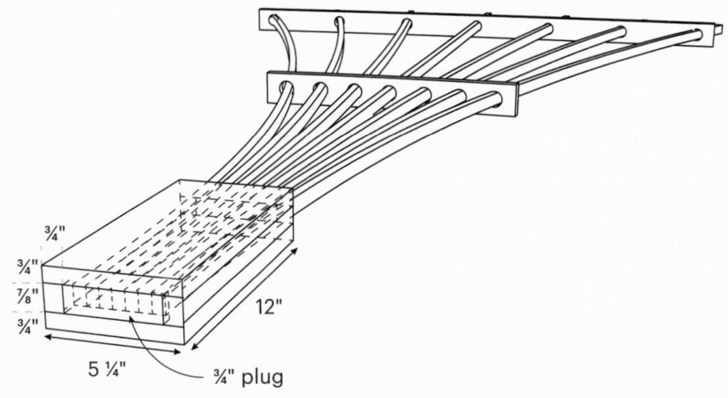

STEP 1

Laying Out the Horizontal Pieces

Select a piece of pine and cut it into two pieces measuring ¾" × 2" × 44" and ¾" × 2" × 17". **(fig. 1)** Save the leftover wood for the base sides.

Measure in ¼" from each end. Using the miter saw, cut a 45-degree angle. **(fig. 2)**

STEP 2

Drilling the Holes

Lay out the hole locations as shown in **figure 3**. Use the 1" spade bit to drill through the wood at each location. (See **diagram B** on page 118.)

> **HELPFUL HINT:** To avoid drilling into your work surface, place scrap wood underneath the piece. **(fig. 4)**

STEP 3

Preparing the Vertical Pieces

Rip and crosscut seven pieces of pine, each measuring ½" × ¾" × 84".

Measure in ¼" on each end of the pieces. Using the miter saw, cut along the marks to create points as shown in **figure 5**.

STEP 4

Building the Base

Select two pieces of pine. Cut two ¾" × 5 ½" × 12" pieces, two ¾" × ⅞" × 12" pieces, and one ¾" × ⅞" × 3" piece.

Align the three ¾" × ⅞" pieces as shown in **figure 6**.

Apply glue and use a brush to spread it evenly. Use a damp cloth to remove any excess glue that squeezes out. **(fig. 7)**

Measure 1" from each end of the ¾" × ⅞" pieces. Countersink and screw the pieces together using 1 ¼" deck screws.

Apply glue, and then attach the backpiece. **(figs. 8–9)** When attaching the backpiece, measure in 2" from each end. Countersink and screw the pieces together using 1 ¼" deck screws.

STEP 5

Putting It All Together

Clamp the base upside down to a level surface.

Take the seven vertical pieces and slide them into the base. **(fig. 10)**

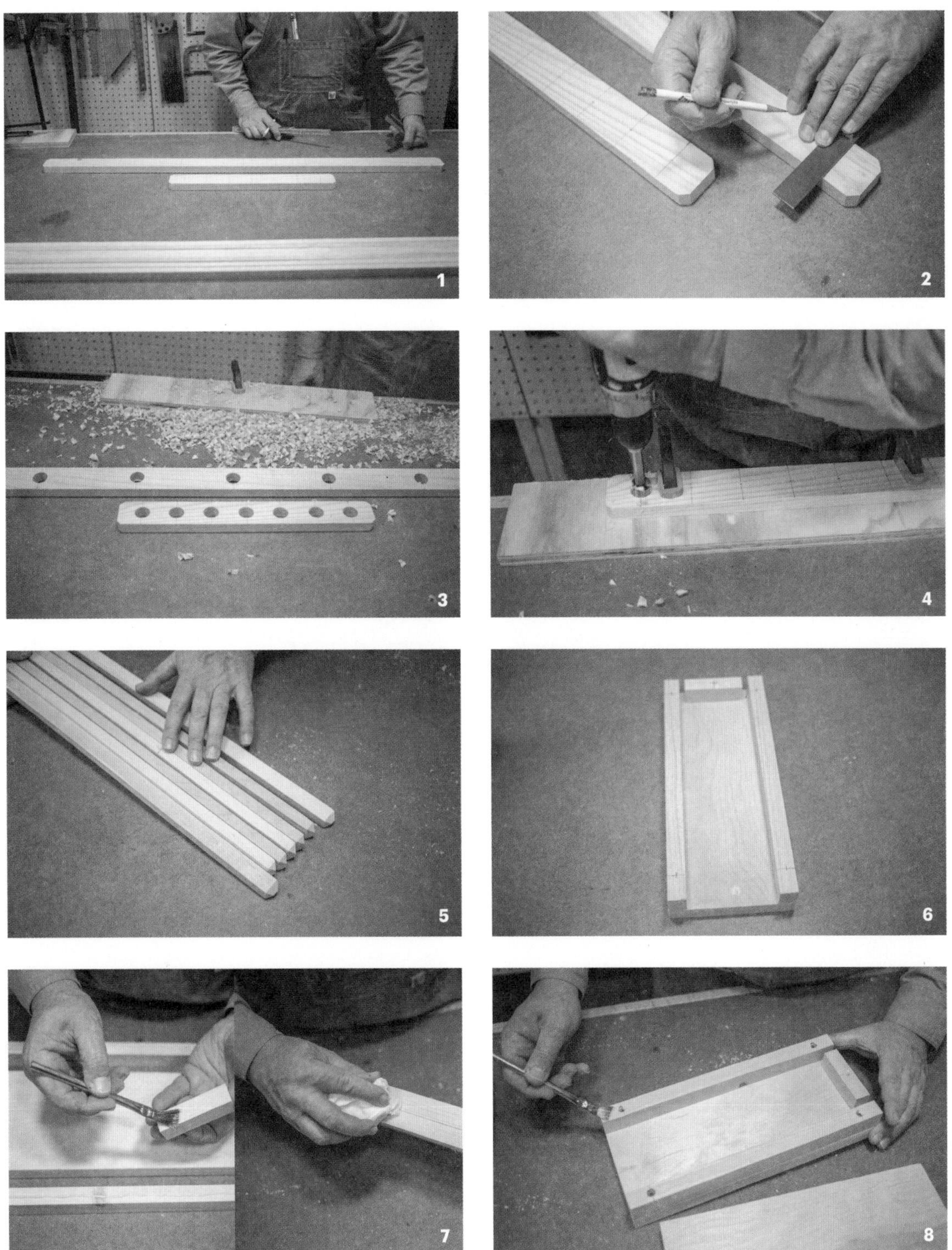

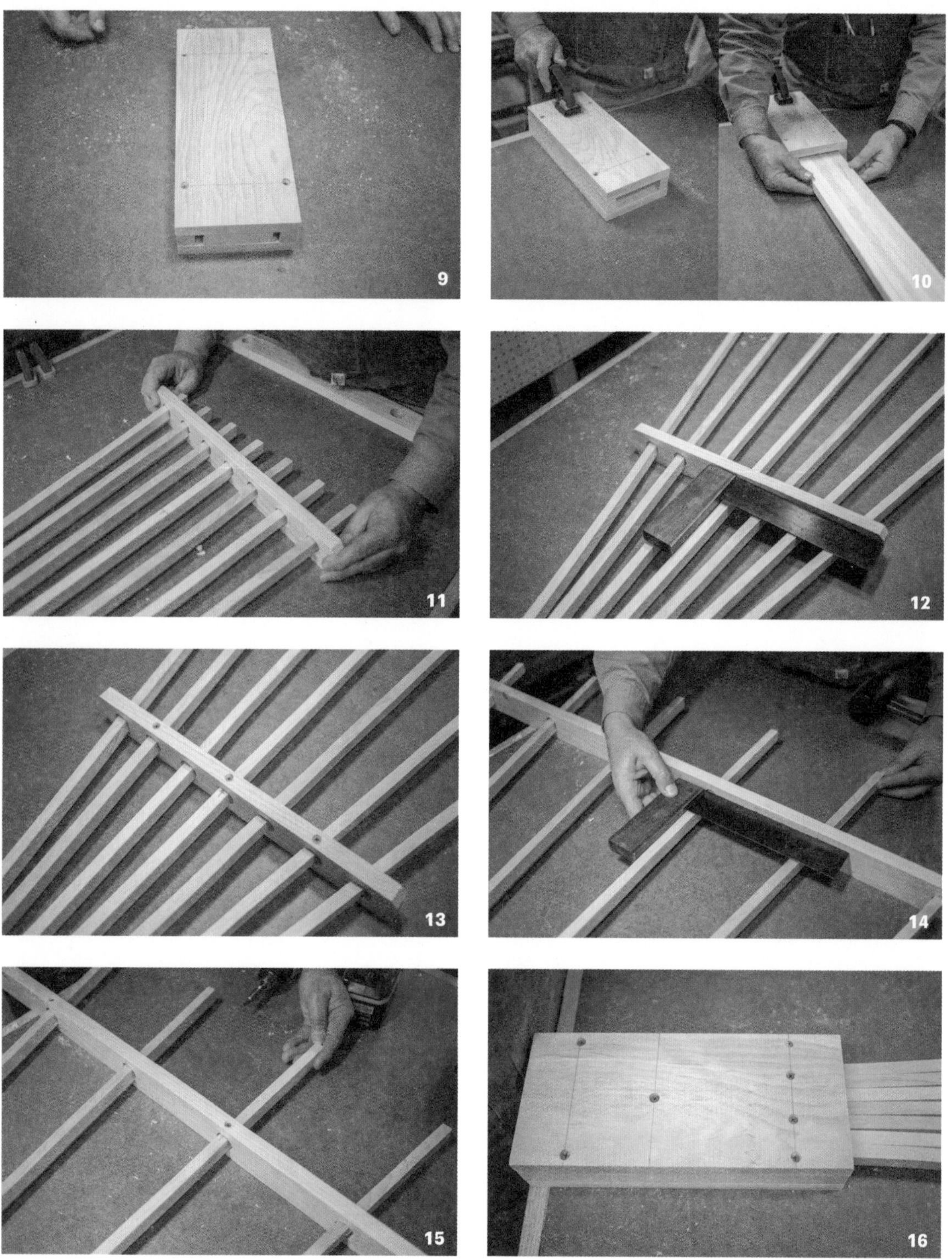
9
10
11
12
13
14
15
16

STEP 6

Setting the Vertical Pieces

Place the ends of the vertical pieces through the holes of the lower horizontal piece. Slide the piece down and stop at 44". **(fig. 11)**

As shown in **figure 12,** use the try square to align the lower horizontal and center vertical pieces.

Attach the lower horizontal piece to three vertical pieces. Countersink and screw with 1 ¼" deck screws. **(fig. 13)**

Take the upper horizontal piece and slide it down 7 ¼" from the top. (See **diagram C** on page 119.) Repeat the instructions to align and attach the pieces. **(figs. 14–15)**

STEP 7

Securing the Vertical Pieces

Attach the vertical pieces to the base. Countersink and screw the pieces together using 1 ¼" deck screws. **(fig. 16)**

NOTES

9.

Plant Stand

This versatile plant stand will look great on your patio, on your porch, or in your sunroom. Its three shelves can support heavy plants and gardening supplies, and are slatted to allow water to drain freely, which is essential for healthy houseplants. Arranging your plants on this stand will add texture and vibrancy to your home. Add a grow light for seed starting and the winter harvesting of herbs and salad greens. You can also use the stand indoors to display decorative items or to organize a space.

Materials Needed

HARDWARE:

- **(28)** 1 ⅝" deck screws
- **(36)** 1 ¼" deck screws
- **(2)** #4 × ⅜" wood screws
- **(1)** box of #18 × ⅝" wire nails

TOOLS:

- Pencils
- Framing square
- Try square
- Hammer
- Small Phillips-head screwdriver
- Tape measure or ruler
- Clamps
- Cordless screw gun or corded drill
- #6 countersink drill bit
- magnetic tip holder with a #2 Phillips-head insert bit
- ⅛" drill bit
- 1/16" drill bit
- Miter saw or miter box
- Table saw (optional)

Diagram A
Materials & Cutting

- **A** Shelf backs (3): ¾" × 3 ½" × 24"
- **B** Shelf fronts (3): ¾" × 3 ½" × 25 ½"
- **C** Shelf 1, sides (2): ¾" × 3 ½" × 12 ¾"
- **D** Shelf 2, sides (2): ¾" × 3 ½" × 16 ¾"
- **E** Shelf 3, sides (2): ¾" × 3 ½" × 20 ¾"
- **F** Back legs (2): ¾" × 2 ½" × 46 ½"
- **G** Front legs (2): ¾" × 2 ½" × 44"
- **H** Top (1): ¾" × 2 ½" × 25 ½"
- **I** Cleats (6): ¾" × 1 ½" × 24"
- **J** Shelf 1, slats (23): ¼" × ¾" × 11 ⅞"
- **K** Shelf 2, slats (23): ¼" × ¾" × 15 ⅞"
- **L** Shelf 3, slats (23): ¼" × ¾" × 19 ⅞"
- **M** Lattice verticals (8): ¼" × ¾" × 8"
- **N** Lattice horizontal (1): ¼" × ¾" × 27"

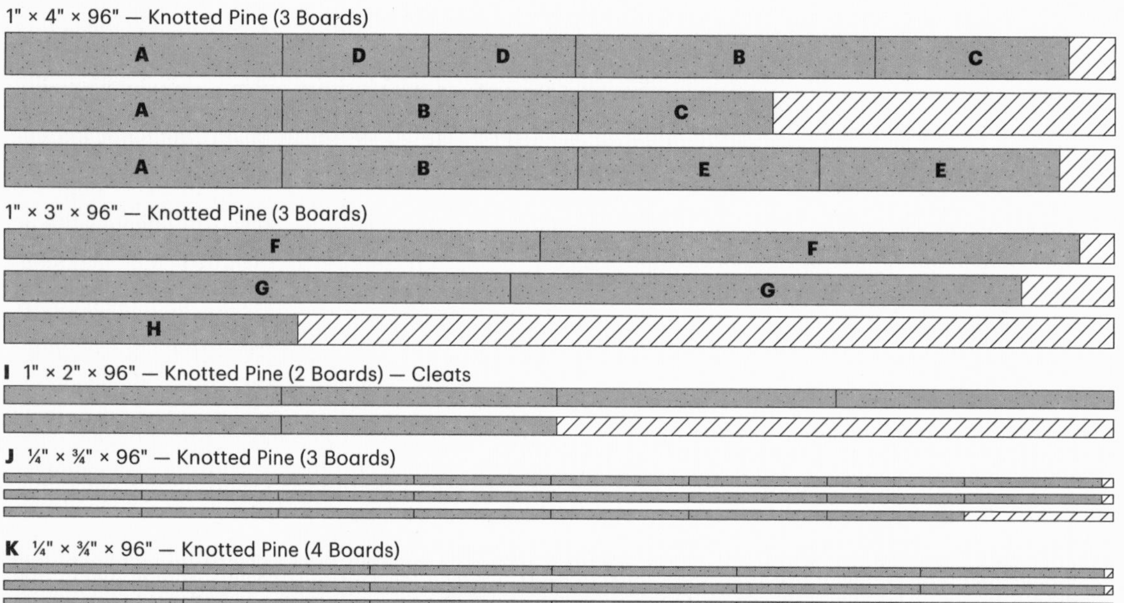

Diagram B
Shelf

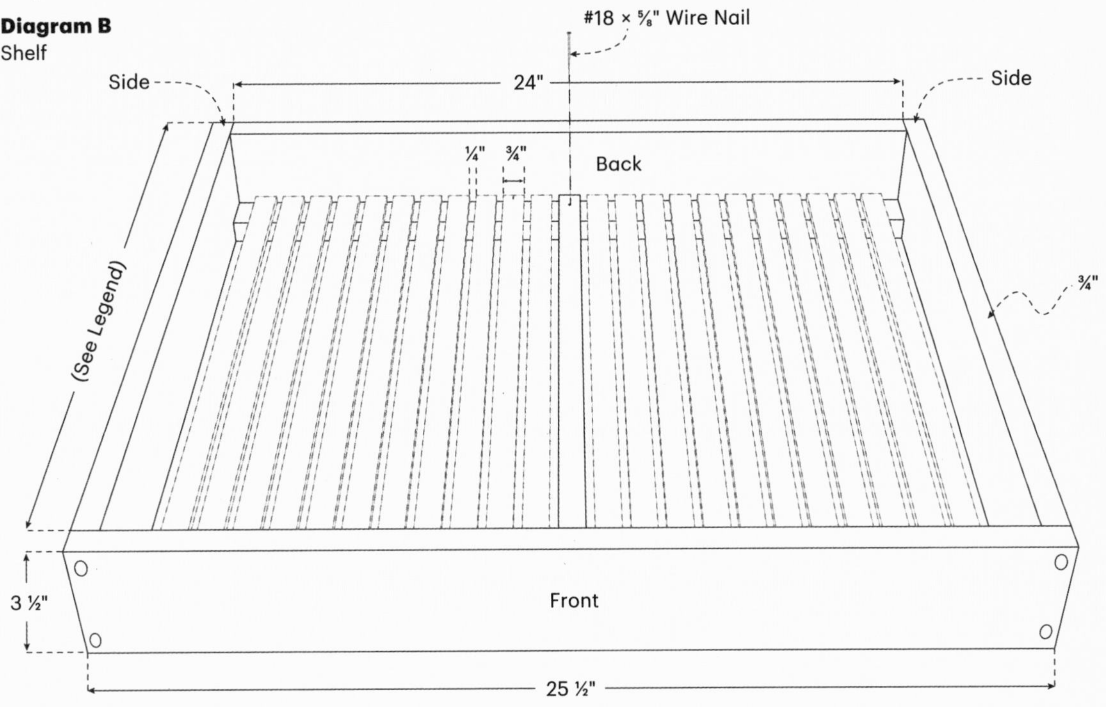

	Side Length	Slat Length
Shelf 1	12 ¾"	11 ⅞"
Shelf 2	16 ¾"	15 ⅞"
Shelf 3	20 ¾"	19 ⅞"

Diagram C
Side

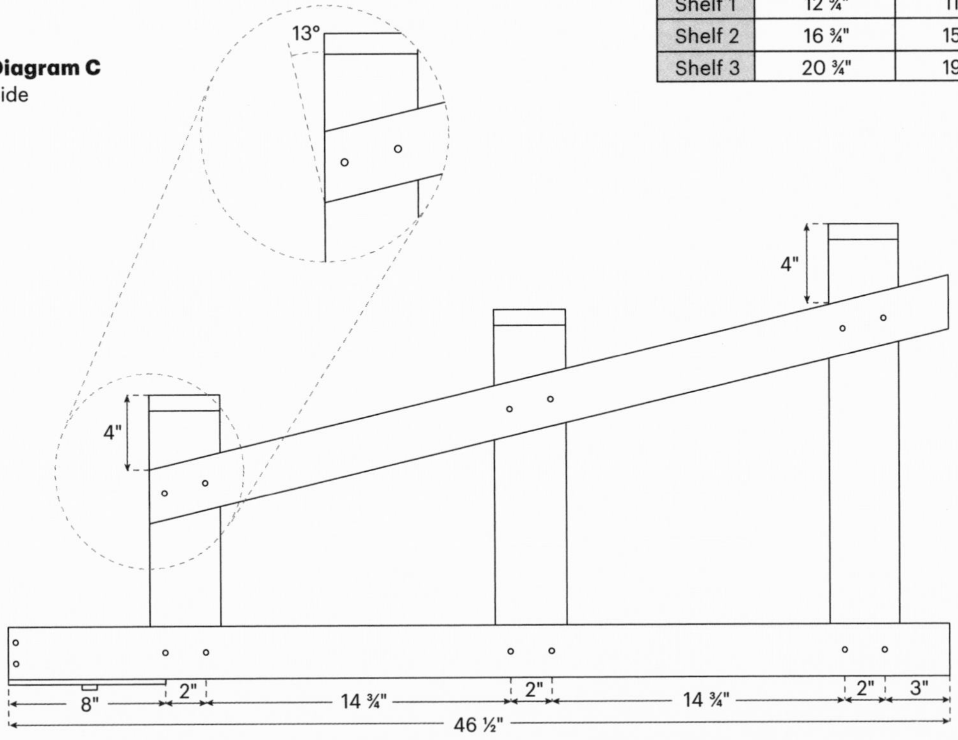

13°
4"
4"
8"
2"
14 ¾"
2"
14 ¾"
2"
3"
46 ½"

STEP 1

Making a Shelf

Select a piece of 1"× 4"× 8' knotted pine, then crosscut one 24" piece and label it "back," two 12 ¾" pieces and label them "sides," and one 25 ½" piece and label it "front."

HELPFUL HINT: Upon leaving a mill, a 1×4's actual dimensions are ¾" × 3 ½" as a result of the drying and planing process. The actual dimensions of the pieces you'll need to cut are ¾" × 3 ½" × 96".

HELPFUL HINT: I recommend cutting all of your shelf pieces at one time to optimize the use of your wood.

STEP 2

Making the Cleats

Select a piece of 1"× 2" × 8' knotted pine and crosscut two 24" pieces. Label each piece "cleat."

STEP 3

Making the Slats and Spacer/Template

To make the slats, select three pieces of ¼" × ¾" × 8' pine and crosscut them into twenty-four individual pieces, each measuring 11 ⅞" long.

Twenty-three of these will be used for the shelf, and one will be used as a spacer to ensure uniform, ¼" spacing when installing the slats.

STEP 4

Preparing the Slats

Predrill the end of each slat to help prevent splitting when nailing them to the cleats. Take one slat and measure from one end ¾" and scribe a line across the width. Measure across that line ⅜" and scribe a mark to indicate where you should predrill. **(fig. 1)**

Drill a 1⁄16" hole at the intersecting point. **(fig. 2)**

HELPFUL HINT: The slat spacer doubles as a predrilling template. After predrilling your first slat, place it on top of a stack of four slats and drill through all of the pieces at once. Use a flat piece of wood to help align your slats, and if you don't want to drill into your work surface, use a piece of scrap wood underneath. **(fig. 3)**

HELPFUL HINT: Use the backer stacker jig while drilling to keep your slats aligned and prevent tear-out. (**figs. 4–5**; see page 26)

1
2
3
4
5
6
7
8

STEP 5

Assembling the Shelf

Take the front, two sides, and back and dry fit them together, making sure that your assembly orientation is correct. **(fig. 6)**

Lay out your drilling points by measuring in ⅜" from the end of the front board and scribe a line across with the try square. Measure ¾" in from both ends of that line and scribe a mark. **(fig. 7)**

Align the pieces you are connecting (the front and left sides in this example), take your drill with the #6 countersink bit, and drill two holes at your first connection. **(fig. 8)**

At the same connection, predrill each hole with the ⅛" drill bit. **(fig. 9)** Take your screw gun with the #2 Phillips bit and insert two 1 ⅝" deck screws into the holes. **(fig. 10)**

Repeat the same procedure at each connection point: align the pieces, countersink, predrill, and insert deck screws.

HELPFUL HINT: Start screws with your fingers first.

STEP 6

Installing the Cleats

Dry fit the cleats, one in front and one in the back. The 2" wide side should be flush with the bottom of the shelf.

Rest the shelf on its front, measure in 3" from each end of the cleat, and scribe a line across the 1" side. Measure across that line ½", and then scribe a mark.

Take your drill and, with the #6 countersink bit, drill a hole into the cleat. Then predrill each hole with the ⅛" drill bit, and insert two 1 ¼" deck screws into each cleat. **(fig. 11)**

Repeat the same procedure at each connection point: align the pieces, countersink, predrill, and insert deck screws.

HELPFUL HINT: If you plan on putting heavy plants on the bottom shelf, you may want to add a support member located under the middle of the slats. Cut a piece of wood to ¾" × 1 ½ × 24" and place it in the same orientation as your cleats. Find the midpoint between the front and back cleats and attach the support member from the outside of the sidepieces. Countersink, predrill, and attach with two 1 ⅝" deck screws.

STEP 7

Attaching the Slats

Measure 12" to the center point of each cleat and scribe a line across the 2" side. **(fig. 12)**

When making your marks on the cleats, use the try square to extend them up the back- and frontpieces. **(fig. 13)** This will help when aligning your center slat.

Take one slat and center it on your mark, using the try square to align it. Use the small hammer to attach the slat with two #18 × ⅝" wire nails. **(fig. 14)**

Place your slat spacer in the upright position next to the center slat and align the next slat. **(fig. 15)** Repeat this procedure of aligning and attaching for all the slats.

Building the second and third shelves will require the same instructions as shown in steps 1–7. The only parts that will change from shelf to shelf are the side and slat lengths. (See legend in **diagram B** on page 127.)

9

10

11

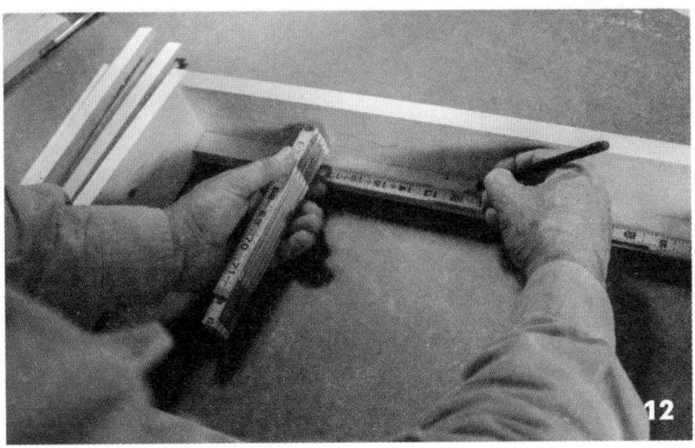

12

How to Make a Predrilling Jig

I used a cutoff piece of 1"× 4"× 6" pine and screwed a piece of ¼" × 1 ½" × 6" stock to it. **(fig. 16)** As shown in **figure 17**, the ¼" stock overhangs and acts as a stop when placing the jig over the piece you are drilling into. This is quite useful when assembling the shelf.

Lay out your drilling points by measuring in ⅜" from the end of the board and scribe a line across the piece with the try square. Measure and scribe along this line at ¾" and 2 ¾".

Take all of your pieces and dry fit them, making sure you assembly orientation is correct. Then mark an *X* everywhere you will be drilling with your jig. **(fig. 18)**

STEP 8

Building the Front and Back Legs

Select a piece of 1"× 3"× 8' knotted pine, and measure and crosscut it into two 46 ½" long pieces.

Label each piece "back leg."

Select a piece of 1"× 3"× 8' knotted pine, measure and crosscut it into two 44" pieces. Label each piece "front leg."

Take the frontpieces and cut a 13-degree angle on one end of each piece. (See **diagram C** on page 127.)

STEP 9

Making Spacer Blocks

> **HELPFUL HINT:** Spacer blocks, sometimes known as memory sticks, are a great way to speed up the assembly process.

Select a piece of 1"× 2"× 8' pine and cut four spacer blocks to 7 ¼", 13 ¼", 13 ¼", and 2 ¼". Label each block as #1–4, accordingly. See **figure 19** for placement.

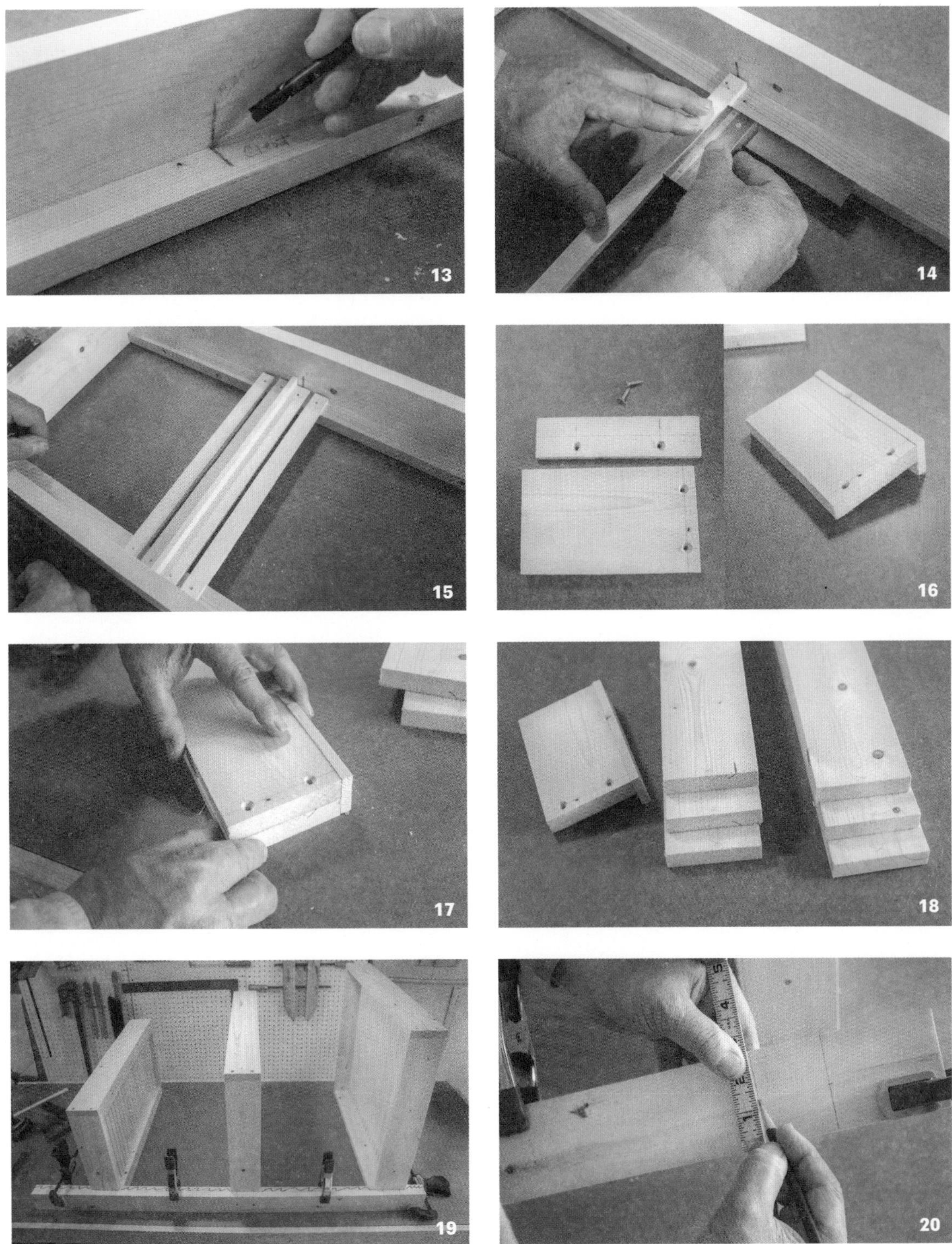
13
14
15
16
17
18
19
20

STEP 10

Connecting the Shelves

Take a back leg piece and place it on its edge on a level surface. Position the shelves and spacer blocks in the correct orientation.

Starting at the top of the leg, measure and scribe at 8", 10", 24 ¾", 26 ¾", 41 ½", and 43 ½" along the piece.

At each mark, use the try square to scribe a line across the piece. Measure and scribe along these lines intersecting marks at 1 ½". **(fig. 20)**

Before you connect the shelves, use the try square to make sure the shelf and back leg pieces are squared off, then countersink, predrill with an ⅛" drill bit, and insert two 1 ¼" deck screws at each connection with a #2 Phillips bit. **(figs. 21–22)**

Repeat the instructions for both back legs.

STEP 11

Positioning the Front Legs

With the back leg installation complete, measure and scribe a mark 4" back from the front faces of shelves #1 and #3. These marks will help when positioning the front leg pieces. **(figs. 23–24)**

Take a front leg piece with the 13-degree angle cut and position it flush to shelf #1, aligning it with the 4" mark on the top of the shelf. Align the lower part of the front leg with the 4" mark on the top of shelf #3. Hold the leg in place with two clamps. **(fig. 25)**

HELPFUL HINT: Use your try square to help align your side-/frontpiece to the marks. **(fig. 26)**

With the leg in place, take spacer block #4 and attach it with a clamp to the bottom of the leg, scribe a line along the 13-degree angle, unclamp the spacer, and trim off the excess. Reattach to the front leg piece and secure it with clamps.

Use the framing square to transfer your drill points from one of the back legs to the front leg. Align the framing square on each point and extend a line across the front legs. **(fig. 27)**

Measure across the line and scribe a mark at 1 ¼", countersink, predrill with the ⅛" drill bit, and insert two 1 ¼" deck screws at each connection. **(figs. 28–29)**

21

22

23

24

25

26

27

28

29

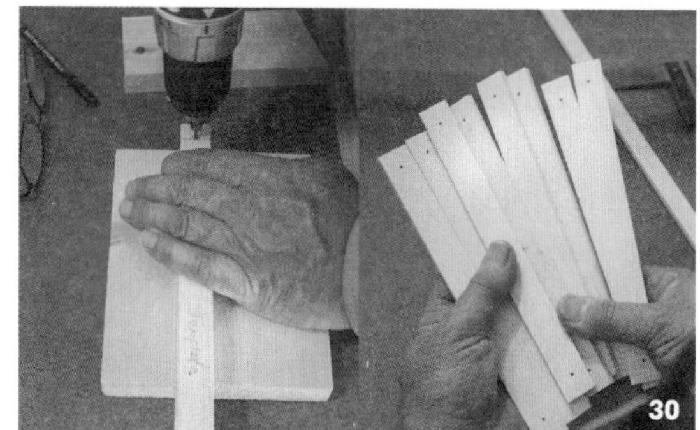
30

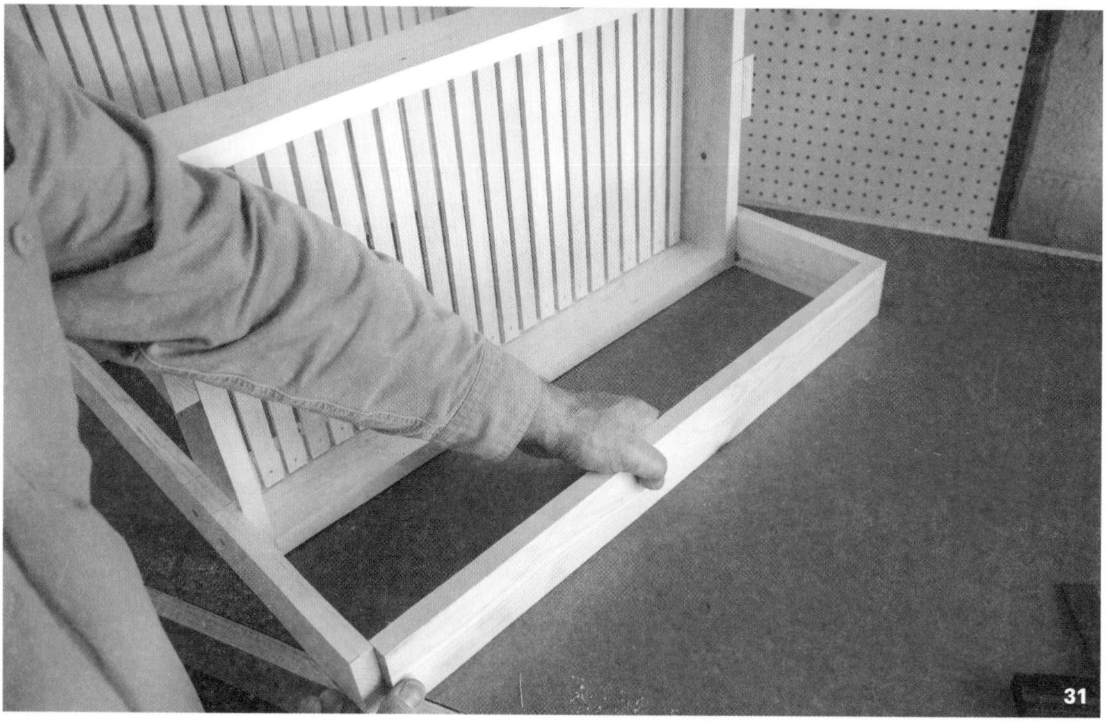

31

32

33

Take your second front leg and repeat the instructions. When attaching your last front leg to your stand, align the piece on the marks and clamp in place. Attach a single screw to the top shelf and gently stand the project up on a level surface to see if it stands correctly. If not, loosen the bottom clamp and adjust the leg until it stands evenly.

Retighten the clamp and attach the rest of the screws.

STEP 12

Making the Top and Lattice Pieces

Select a piece of 1"× 3"× 8' knotted pine and crosscut it to 25 ½" and label it "top."

Select a piece of ¼" × ¾" × 8' pine and crosscut it into eight pieces measuring 8" and one measuring 27". Label the 8" pieces "lattice verticals" and the 27" piece "lattice horizontal." From the same piece of pine, cut one more piece measuring 2 ⅞" long and label it "lattice spacer."

Take the lattice spacer and scribe a mark at 1 7/16" from one end and use the try square to make a line across the piece. Predrill your lattice pieces by using the slat/spacer template. **(fig. 30)**

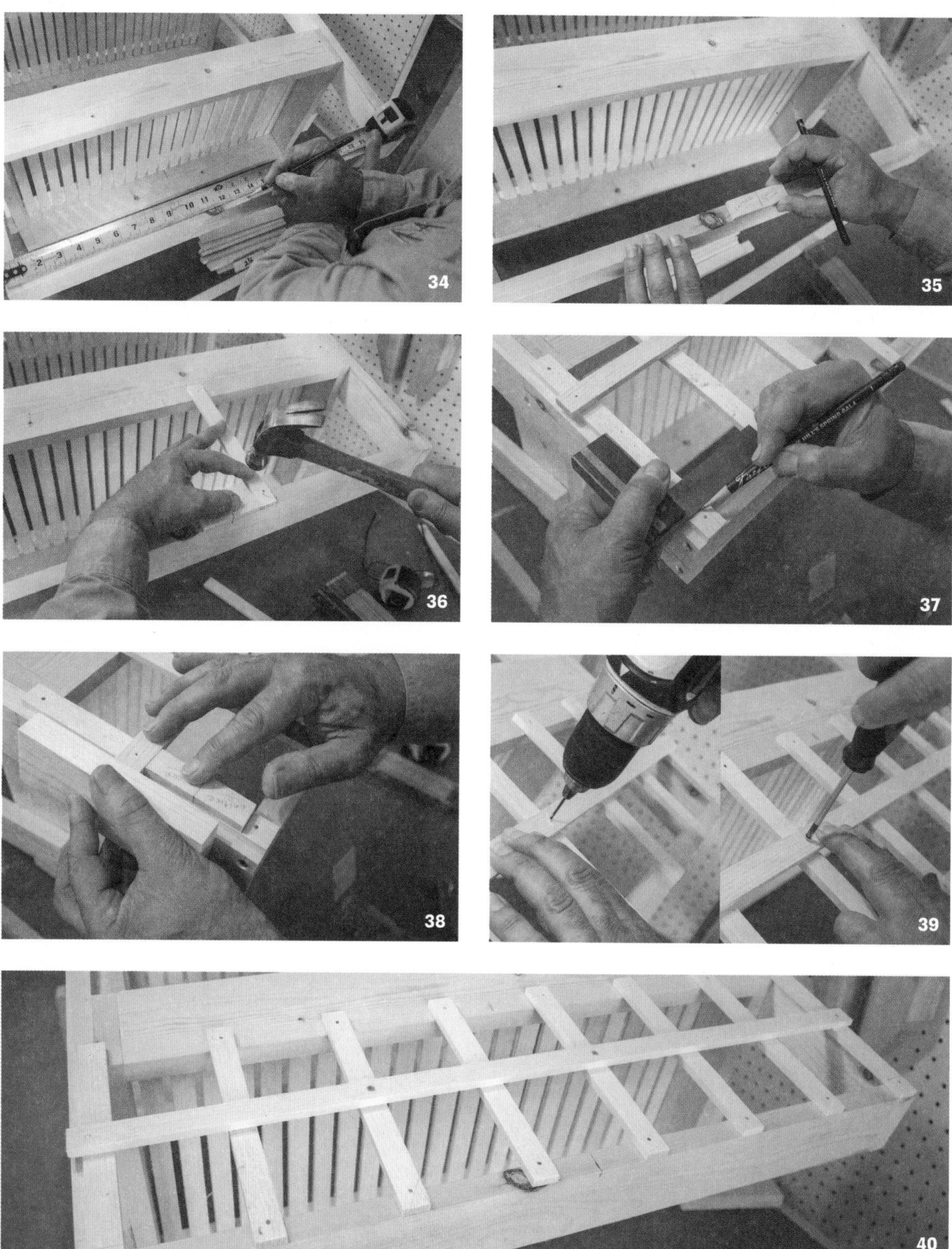
34
35
36
37
38
39
40

STEP 13

Attaching the Top and Lattice Back

Take your top piece and dry fit it between the top of the two back legs. **(fig. 31)** Measure ⅜" from the top of the back leg pieces and use the try square to scribe a line across. **(fig. 32)**

Measure and scribe along this line at ¾" and 1 ¾". **(fig. 33)**

Take a drill with the #6 countersink bit and drill two holes at your first connection, then predrill with the ⅛" drill bit. Take your screw gun with the #2 Phillips bit and insert two 1 ⅝" deck screws at each connection. Repeat the instructions for the other side.

Place the plant stand down on a level surface so that it is now resting on its front face. Measure and scribe a center mark on the back of the top piece. **(fig. 34)** Take your lattice spacer and center it on this mark. **(fig. 35)** Place a piece of lattice next to the spacer, using the try square to align it. Attach the lattice by hammering in two ⅝" wire nails. **(fig. 36)** Repeat this procedure until all eight vertical lattice pieces are installed.

To attach the horizontal lattice piece, measure and scribe a mark ¾" down from the tops of the two outer lattice pieces with the try square and scribe a line across these two pieces. **(fig. 37)** Align the lattice spacer to that line and position the horizontal lattice piece. **(fig. 38)** Secure the piece by hammering a #18 × ⅝" wire nail into each of the two outer lattice pieces.

HELPFUL HINT: To keep the ends of the horizontal lattice piece flush with the side- and backpieces, use a block of wood to align it.

To secure the vertical lattice pieces to the horizontal one, take a drill with the 1⁄16" drill bit and predrill two holes. At each intersecting point, insert a #4 × ⅜" wood screw with the Phillips-head screwdriver. **(figs. 39–40)**

NOTES

10.

Garden Chair

Turn your garden into a restful retreat with this comfortable chair. Its high back design and sturdy construction make it relaxing to sit in. The bottom shelf provides additional storage for newspapers, books, and snacks. The natural wood will age and weather over time. If you're looking to enhance or add seating to your garden or patio, this chair will give you an easy solution.

Materials Needed

HARDWARE:

(1) 1 lb. box of 1 ½" deck screws

(1) 1 lb. box of 2 ½" deck screws

(1) piece of 1 ½" diameter PVC pipe (2"–3" long)

(1) sheet of 80-grit sandpaper

(2) sheets of 220-grit sandpaper

TOOLS:

Pencil

Try square

Phillips-head screwdriver

Tape measure

Clamps

Jigsaw or coping saw

Cordless screw gun or corded drill

#6 countersink drill bit

Magnetic tip holder with a #2 Phillips insert bit

⅛" drill bit

Miter saw or miter box (optional)

Table saw (optional)

Diagram A
Materials & Cutting

A Back slats (5): ¾" × 3 ½" × 43 ½"
B Seat slats (5): ¾" × 3 ½" × 17 ¾"
C Base slats (5): ¾" × 3 ½" × 24"
D Middle/back legs (4): 1" × 2 ¼" × 26 ¼"
E Arms (2): ¾" × 3 ½" × 17"
F Leg cleats (6): 1" × 2 ¼" × 3 ½"
G Back supports (3): 1" × 1 ½" × 19"
H Seat supports (2): 1" × 1 ½" × 19"
I Crossbar: 1" × 2 ¼" × 21 ¼"
J Back side rails (2): 1" × 2 ¼" × 43 ½"
K Seat side rails (2): 1" × 2 ¼" × 17 ¾"
L Front legs (2): 1" × 2 ¼" × 18 ½"
M Seat attaching supports (2): 1" × 2 ¼" × 19"
N Base side rails (2): 1" × 2 ¼" × 24"
O Base supports (2): 1" × 1 ½" × 19"

1" × 4" × 96" — Knotted Pine (5 boards)

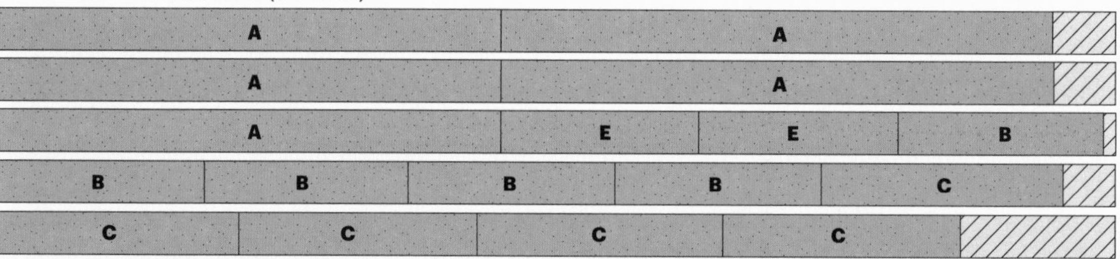

1" × 2 ¼" × 96" — Knotted Pine (5 boards)

D D D F F F F F
D I K K F
J J
M M N N
L L

1" × 1 ½" × 96" — Knotted Pine (2 boards)

G G G H H
O O

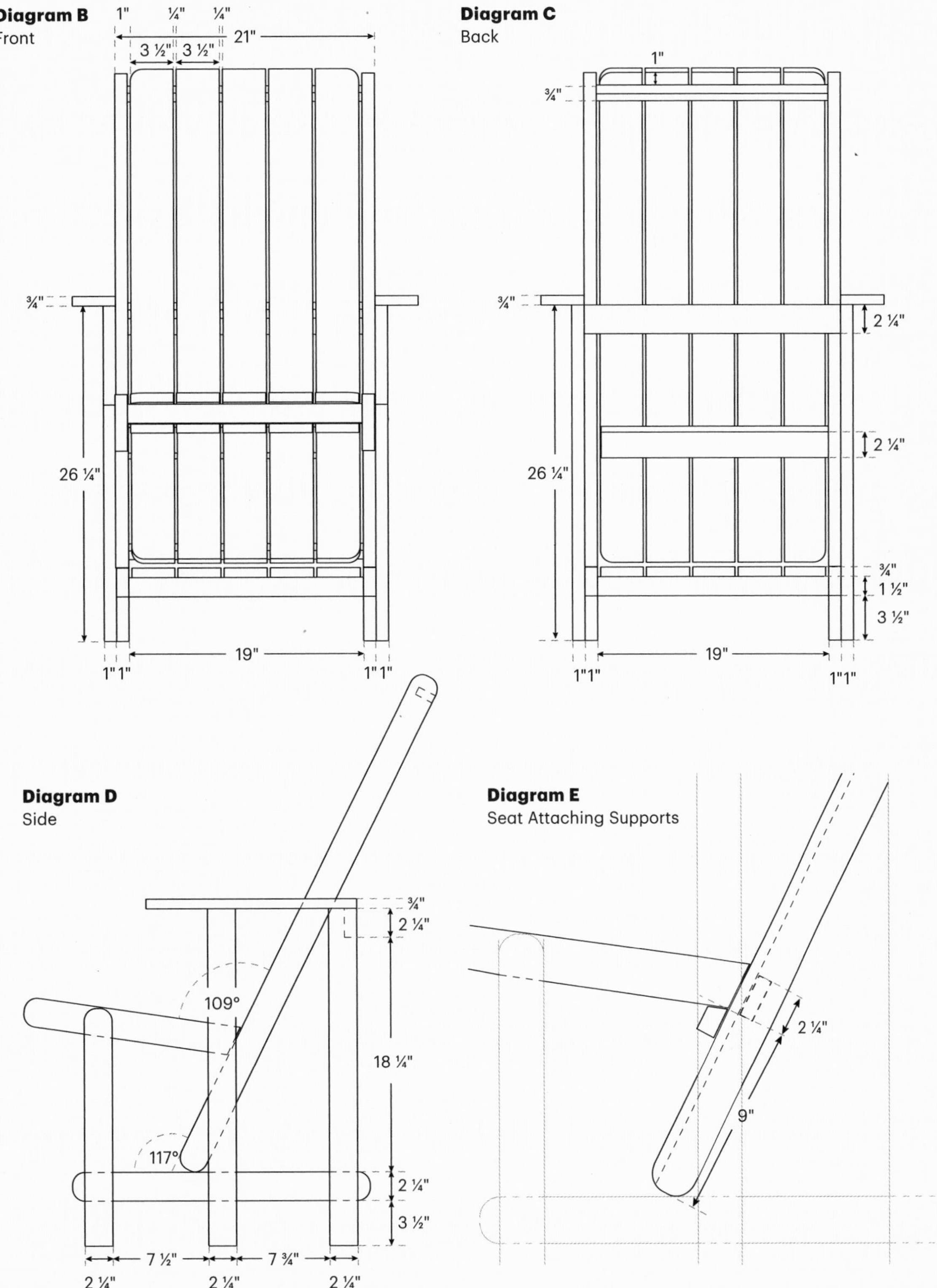
Diagram B
Front
1"
¼"
¼"
21"
3 ½"
3 ½"
¾"
26 ¼"
19"
1" 1"
1" 1"
Diagram C
Back
1"
¾"
¾"
2 ¼"
2 ¼"
26 ¼"
¾"
1 ½"
3 ½"
19"
1"1"
1"1"
Diagram D
Side
¾"
2 ¼"
109°
18 ¼"
117°
2 ¼"
3 ½"
7 ½"
7 ¾"
2 ¼"
2 ¼"
2 ¼"
Diagram E
Seat Attaching Supports
2 ¼"
9"

STEP 1

Making the Back Side Rails

Select and cut two pieces of pine, each measuring 1" × 2 ¼" × 43 ½".

As shown in **figure 1**, use the piece of 1 ½" PVC pipe to create curved corners.

Use the jigsaw or coping saw and cut along the lines as shown in **figure 2**.

Take a piece of 80-grit sandpaper and shape the edges. **(fig. 3)**

> **HELPFUL HINT:** When making shapes with a jigsaw or coping saw, leave the line visible when you cut the wood, then use a piece of sandpaper to shape the wood to the line.

STEP 2

Making the Back Supports

Select and cut three pieces of pine, each measuring 1" × 1 ½" × 19".

> **HELPFUL HINT:** Make a jig to help create a 1" overhang as shown in **figure 4**.

STEP 3

Assembling the Frame

Using a jig and the try square, align the pieces. Attach them by countersinking and screwing with 1 ½" deck screws. **(figs. 5–6)**

STEP 4

Making the Slats

Select and cut five pieces of pine, each measuring ¾" × 3 ½" × 43 ½".

Use the piece of PVC pipe to create rounded corners on two of the slats. **(fig. 7)**

> **HELPFUL HINT:** Create a T jig to help make sure the connections are consistent and secure when you're screwing the slats to the rails. **(fig. 8**; see page 23**)**

1
2
3
4
5
6
7
8

STEP 5

Attaching the Slats

Lay the slats out on a level work surface and position the frame on top of them.

As shown in **figure 9**, put ¼" spacers in between the slats.

Using a jig, predrill each hole with the ⅛" bit, then countersink and attach with two 1 ½" deck screws. **(figs. 10–12)**

STEP 6

Making the Seat Side Rails

Select two pieces of pine, each measuring 1" × 2 ¼" × 17 ¾".

Cut a 20-degree angle on one end of each piece, leaving the pieces measuring 17 ½" long.

On the front edge of each piece, use the piece of PVC pipe to create curved corners.

STEP 7

Making the Seat Supports

Select and cut two pieces of pine, each measuring 1" × 1 ½" × 19".

STEP 8

Assembling the Seat Frame

Use a jig and the try square to align the pieces.

Attach the pieces by predrilling with the ⅛" bit, countersinking, and screwing with 1 ½" deck screws.

STEP 9

Making the Seat Slats

Select and cut five pieces of pine, each measuring ¾" × 3 ½" × 17 ¾".

On each end, cut a 20-degree angle, leaving the pieces measuring 17 ½" long. **(fig. 13)**

Use the piece of PVC pipe to round the corners.

STEP 10

Attaching the Seat Slats

Using a jig, predrill each hole with the ⅛" bit, then countersink and screw with 1 ½" deck screws. **(figs. 14–15)**

9
10
11
12
13
14
15
16

STEP 11

Making the Seat Attaching Supports

See **diagram E** on page 145.

Select and cut a piece of pine measuring 1" × 2 ¼" × 19". On one side of the piece, rip a 20-degree angle.

Position the piece and secure it by countersinking and attaching it with five 1 ½" deck screws. **(fig. 16)**

Select and cut a piece of pine measuring 1" × 2 ¼" × 19". Countersink and secure with five 1 ½" deck screws. **(fig. 17)**

STEP 12

Attaching the Seat to the Back

Create an angle-finding jig. (See page 27.)

Using the jig set to a 20-degree angle, align the seat to the back. **(fig. 18)**

Attach the seat by predrilling with the ⅛" bit, countersinking, and screwing with 3 ½" deck screws. **(figs. 19–20)**

STEP 13

Making the Base Side Rails

Select and cut two pieces of pine, each measuring 1" × 2 ¼" × 24".

Use the piece of PVC pipe to create rounded corners.

Using the jigsaw or coping saw, cut along the lines.

HELPFUL HINT: When cutting with a jigsaw, cut next to the layout lines, then sand the piece up to the line.

STEP 14

Making the Base Supports

Select and cut two pieces of pine, each measuring 1" × 1 ½" × 19".

STEP 15

Assembling the Base Frame

Using a jig and the try square, align the pieces. Attach the pieces by predrilling with the ⅛" bit, countersinking, and screwing with 1 ½" deck screws. **(fig. 21)**

STEP 16

Making the Base Slats

Select and cut five pieces of pine, each measuring ¾" × 3 ½" × 24".

Use the piece of PVC pipe to create rounded corners.

17
18
19
20
21
22
23
24

25
26
27
28
29
30
31
32

STEP 17

Attaching the Slats

Lay the slats out on a level work surface. Place ¼" spacers in between the slats and position the frame on top of the slats.

Using a jig, predrill with the ⅛" bit, countersink, and screw with 1 ½" deck screws. **(figs. 22–24)**

STEP 18

Making the Legs

Select and cut six pieces of pine, four measuring 1" × 2 ¼" × 26 ¼" and two measuring 1" × 2 ¼" × 18 ½".

STEP 19

Attaching Cleats to the Legs

Select and cut six pieces of pine, each measuring 1" × 2 ¼" × 3 ½".

HELPFUL HINT: Create a jig that will help you make consistent and secure connections when you're attaching the pieces together. **(fig. 25)**

Using a jig, predrill two holes with the ⅛" bit, then countersink and attach with 1 ½" deck screws. **(fig. 26)**

Use the jig to align the pieces when attaching the cleat to the leg. **(fig. 27)**

STEP 20

Attaching the Legs

On a level work surface, position the base on top of the legs. **(fig. 28)**

As shown in **figures 29–30**, use a jig to leave a 1" overhang at the leading edge and back of the base.

Using the try square, align the legs to the base. **(fig. 31)**

Attach the legs by countersinking two staggered holes. Screw the pieces together with two 1 ½" deck screws at each connecting point. **(fig. 32)**

When completed, secure the base on a level surface and adjust as needed.

STEP 21

Making the Crossbar

Select and cut a piece of pine measuring 1" × 2 ¼" × 21 ¼".

As shown in **figure 33**, use a piece of scrap wood to hold the crossbar in place while attaching.

Attach the crossbar by predrilling with the ⅛" bit, countersinking, and screwing in 1 ½" deck screws.

STEP 22

Attaching the Seat to the Base

Position the seat on the base as shown in **figure 34**.

Using the angle jig set to a 27-degree angle, align the seat and base. **(fig. 35)**

HELPFUL HINT: Clamp two pieces of scrap wood, each measuring 8 ½" long, to the front legs as shown in **figure 36**. These pieces of scrap wood will act as an extra set of hands to hold the piece in place.

Using the try square, align the back leg with the seat as shown in **figure 37**.

Attach the seat to the back leg by predrilling with the ⅛" bit, countersinking, and screwing with a 1 ½" deck screw. **(fig. 38)**

To attach the seat to the middle leg, predrill with the ⅛" bit, countersink, and screw in two 1 ½" deck screws. **(fig. 39)**

Using an angle jig set to a 20-degree angle, position the seat to the base, as shown in **figure 40**.

When the seat is set to the 20-degree angle, attach wherever the legs intersect the seat. **(fig. 41)**

STEP 23

Making and Attaching the Arms

Select and cut two pieces of pine, each measuring ¾" × 3 ½" × 17".

Use the piece of PVC to create curved corners, and, with the jigsaw or coping saw, cut along the lines.

When positioning the arms, leave a ¾" overhang at the back of the arm, as shown in **figure 42**.

Attach the arms by predrilling with the ⅛" bit then countersinking and screwing with two 1 ½" deck screws.

33

34

35

36

37

38

39

40

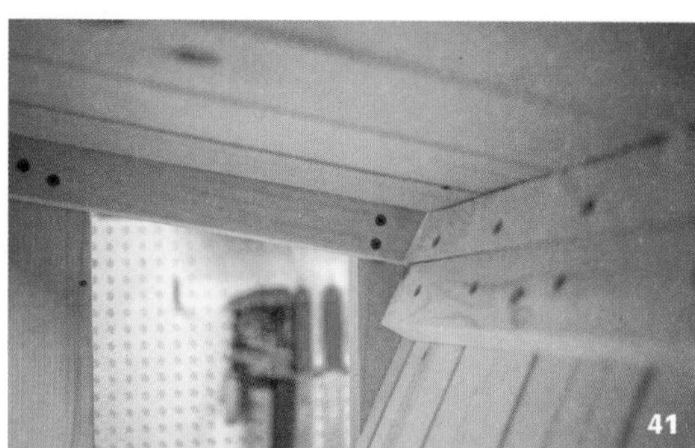
41

42

NOTES

11.

Cold Frame

A cold frame is a simple structure that you can use to generate and maintain an optimally warm and humid environment for growing plants, and to help extend your growing season through the colder months. Positioning your cold frame toward the south will allow its translucent cover to absorb as much daytime radiation from the sun as possible, creating a small greenhouse. You can use this system to start seedlings that can later be transplanted to your summer garden, and to keep your fruits and veggies thriving throughout the year. You should select a location that is easily accessible, so that you can check on it regularly. Growing in a cold frame takes time to perfect, but successful seasons are not difficult to accomplish.

Materials Needed

HARDWARE:

(1) 1 lb. box of 1 ½" deck screws

(1) 2" Woodtite fasteners (fifty-pack)

(1) 1 lb. box of 1 ¼" deck screws

(2) ¼" × 2" zinc lag screws

(2) ¼" × ⅜" plastic spacers

(4) ¼" zinc-plated washers

(4) ⅜" × 3" galvanized carriage bolts

(4) ⅜" galvanized washers

(4) ⅜" galvanized nuts

(2) ⅜" × 2 ½" zinc carriage bolts

(2) ⅜" zinc wing nuts

(1) 1 ⅜" × ⅟₁₆" × 48" zinc-plated steel punched flat bar

(2) 3" oil-rubbed bronze-finish door hinges

(2) packs of 24" Suntuf horizontal plastic closure strips

(2) 12' Palruf clear PVC roof panel

(2) sheets of 220-grit sandpaper

TOOLS:

Pencil

Hammer

Try square

Framing square

Phillips-head screwdriver

Tape measure

Hacksaw

Clamps

Utility knife

Shears

Wrench

Jigsaw

Cordless screw gun or corded drill

#6 countersink drill bit

Magnetic tip holder with a #2 Phillips insert bit

1" Forstner bit

⅛" drill bit

½" drill bit

Diagram B
Back

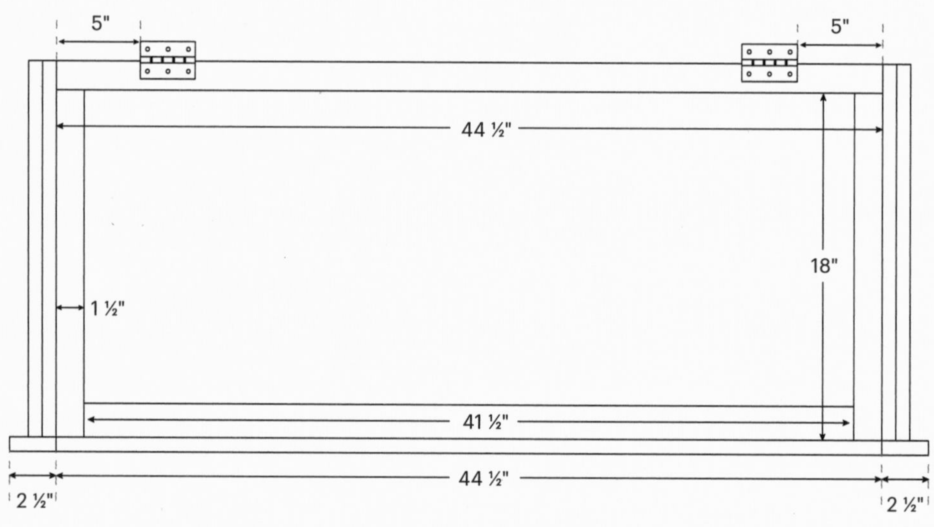

Diagram A
Materials & Cutting

A Lid (3): ¾" × 2 ½" × 43 ½"
B Lid (2): ¾" × 2 ½" × 46"
C Lid (3): ¾" × 2 ½" × 48 ½"
D Lid (4): ¾" × 2 ½" × 19 ¼"
E Side trim vertical (2): ¾" × 2 ½" × 12 ½"
F Side trim horizontal (2): ¾" × 2 ½" × 38 ½"
G Front connection pieces (2): 1 ½" × 1 ½" × 12"
H Front trim vertical (2): ¾" × 2 ½" × 12"
I Front trim horizontal (2): ¾" × 2 ½" × 42 ½"
J Back frame vertical (2): 1 ½" × 1 ½" × 18"
K Back frame horizontal, top: 1 ½" × 1 ½" × 44 ½"
L Back frame horizontal, bottom: 1 ½" × 1 ½" × 41 ½"
M Bottom pieces (2): ¾" × 2 ½" × 46 ½"
N Bottom piece: ¾" × 2 ½" × 49 ½"
O Bottom piece: ¾" × 2 ½" × 44 ½"
P Plywood front: ¾" × 12 ⅝" × 44 ½"
Q Plywood back: ¾" × 19 ⅝" × 44 ½"
R Plywood side: ¾" × 39" × 43 ¾"
S Lid sealer strips (2): ¾" × ¾" × 20 ½"
T Lid sealer strip: ¾" × ¾" × 46"

1" × 3" × 96" — Knotted Pine (10 boards)

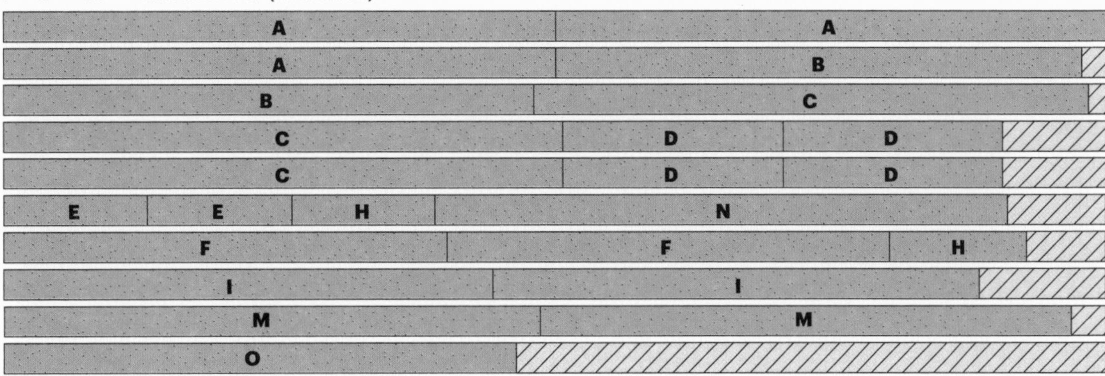

1 ½" × 1 ½" × 96" — Knotted Pine (2 boards)

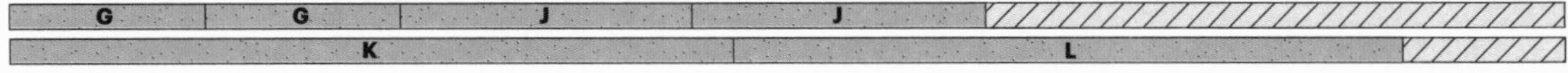

¾" × ¾" × 96" — Knotted Pine (1 board)

¾" × 48" × 96" — Plywood (1 board)

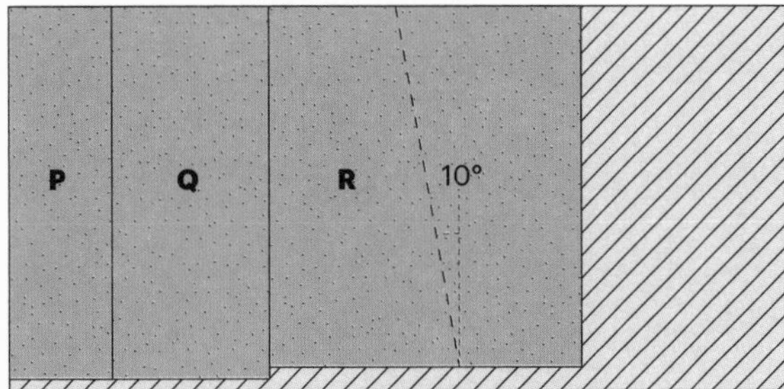

Diagram C
Side

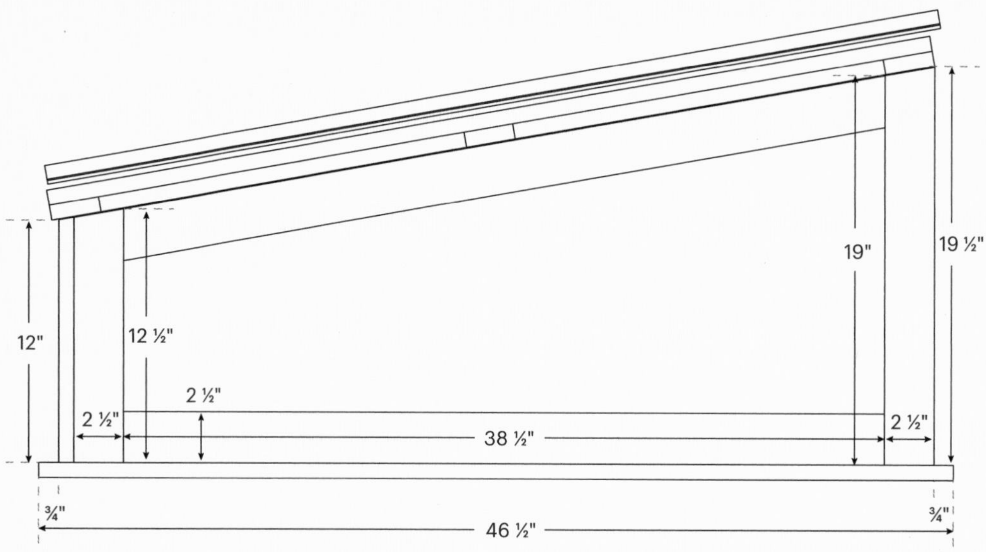

Diagram D
Front

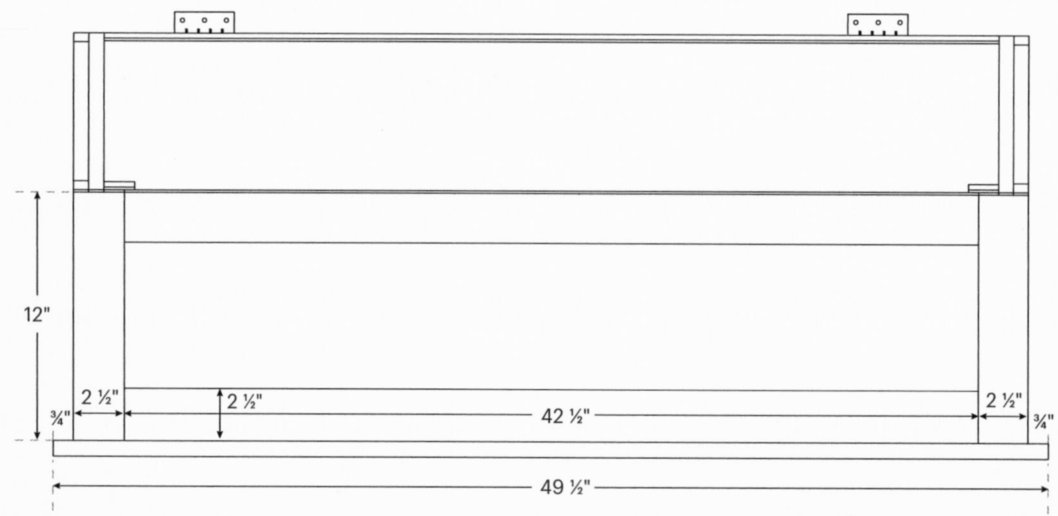

Diagram E
Lid

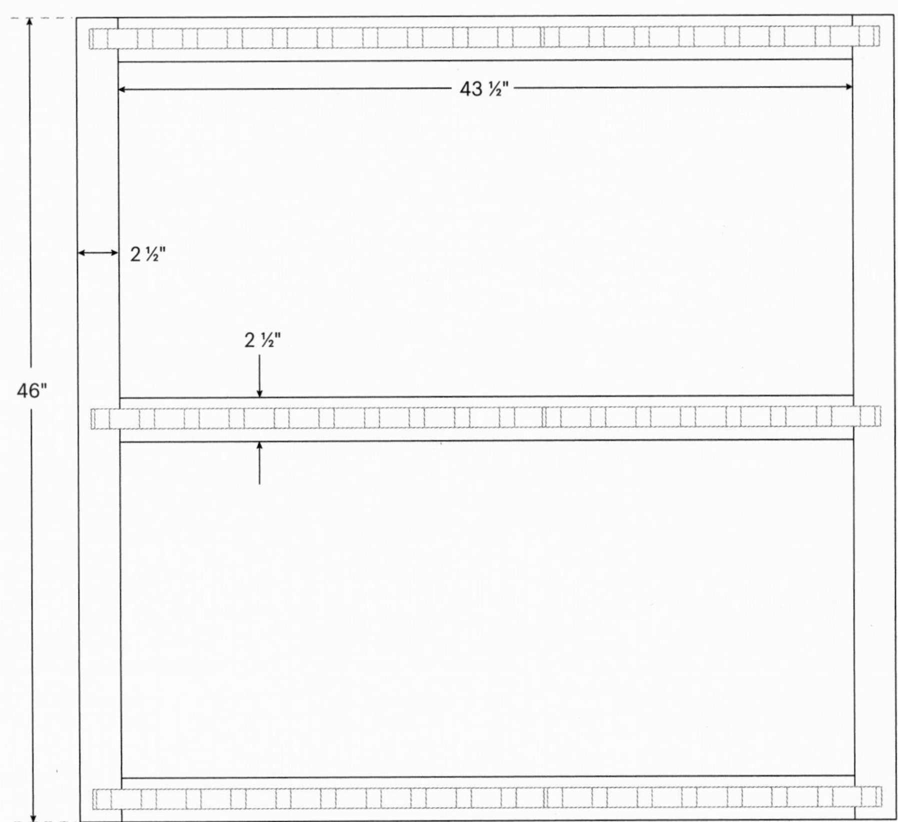

STEP 1

Making the Lid Frame

Select and cut two pieces of pine, each measuring ¾" × 2 ½" × 46".

Select and cut three pieces of pine, each measuring ¾" × 2 ½" × 48 ½".

As shown in **figure 1**, overlap the pieces to create a frame.

HELPFUL HINT: Create an attaching jig, such as in **figure 2**, to help create secure connections when you screw the frame together. (See page 24.)

Place the jig on the pieces, then predrill with the ⅛" bit, countersink, and screw in a 1 ¼" deck screw. **(fig. 3)** Only insert one screw—this will create a hinge.

Use the try square to align the pieces. **(fig. 4)** Now that the pieces are squared off, install the remaining screws.

Select and cut four pieces of pine, each measuring ¾" × 2 ½" × 19 ¼".

Select and cut three pieces of pine, each measuring ¾" × 2 ½" × 43 ½".

Use these pieces as fillers on the frame.

HELPFUL HINT: A great way to speed up any assembly is to use your thumb and pinky finger as a ruler.

Predrill with the ⅛" bit, then countersink and screw with 1 ¼" deck screws. **(fig. 5)**

STEP 2

Installing the PVC Roof

As shown in **figure 6**, install the 24" Suntuf horizontal plastic closure strips onto the frame using 2" Woodtite fasteners.

Lay out the 12' Palruf PVC roof panel on a level surface. With the shears, cut two pieces, each measuring 48" long. **(fig. 7)**

Place both pieces onto the frame, leaving a 1" overhang as shown in **figure 8**.

Attach the roof to the frame with 2" Woodtite fasteners.

9
10
11
12
13
14
15
16

STEP 3

Sealing the Sides of the Roof

Select and cut three pieces of pine, two measuring ¾" × ¾" × 20 ½", and the third measuring ¾" × ¾" × 46".

Fit the two 20 ½" pieces in between the horizontal strips. **(fig. 9)**

As shown in **figures 10–11**, use a utility knife to trim off the connecting tabs on the horizontal strips. This will allow room for the 46" piece of wood.

When all three pieces are in place, attach them by predrilling with the ⅛" bit, countersinking, and screwing with 1 ¼" deck screws. **(fig. 12)**

Finish attaching the PVC roof to the frame with 2" Woodtite fasteners. **(figs. 13–14)**

STEP 4

Making the Sides

Select a piece of plywood and cut it to ¾" × 39" × 43 ¾".

Using the jigsaw, cut the plywood to create two 10-degree angles as shown in **figures 15–16**. (See **diagram C** on page 162.)

STEP 5

Making the Front and Back

Select a piece of plywood measuring ¾" × 33" × 44 ½". Using the jigsaw, cut two pieces, one measuring ¾" × 12 ⅝" × 44 ½" and the other ¾" × 19 ⅝" × 44 ½".

Attach 1 ½" × 1 ½" pine to the two pieces of plywood. Countersink and screw with 1 ½" deck screws, as shown in **figure 17**. This will create a tight seal when you close the lid and also make a stable surface to mount your hinges. (See **diagram B** on page 160.)

Use the jigsaw to cut a 10-degree angle on the top edge of both pieces.

STEP 6

Installing the Front and Back

As shown in **figure 18**, hold the side to the back using clamps. Use a framing square to align the pieces.

Mark the locations of the drilling points. Using the 1" Forstner bit, drill ½" deep into the plywood. Using the ⅜" bit, drill through the plywood and pine. **(figs. 19–21)**

Once the holes are drilled, use ⅜" × 3" galvanized carriage bolts, washers, and nuts to attach the pieces. **(fig. 22)**

HELPFUL HINT: When installing carriage bolts, use a hammer to tap the bolts into place. **(figs. 23–24)**

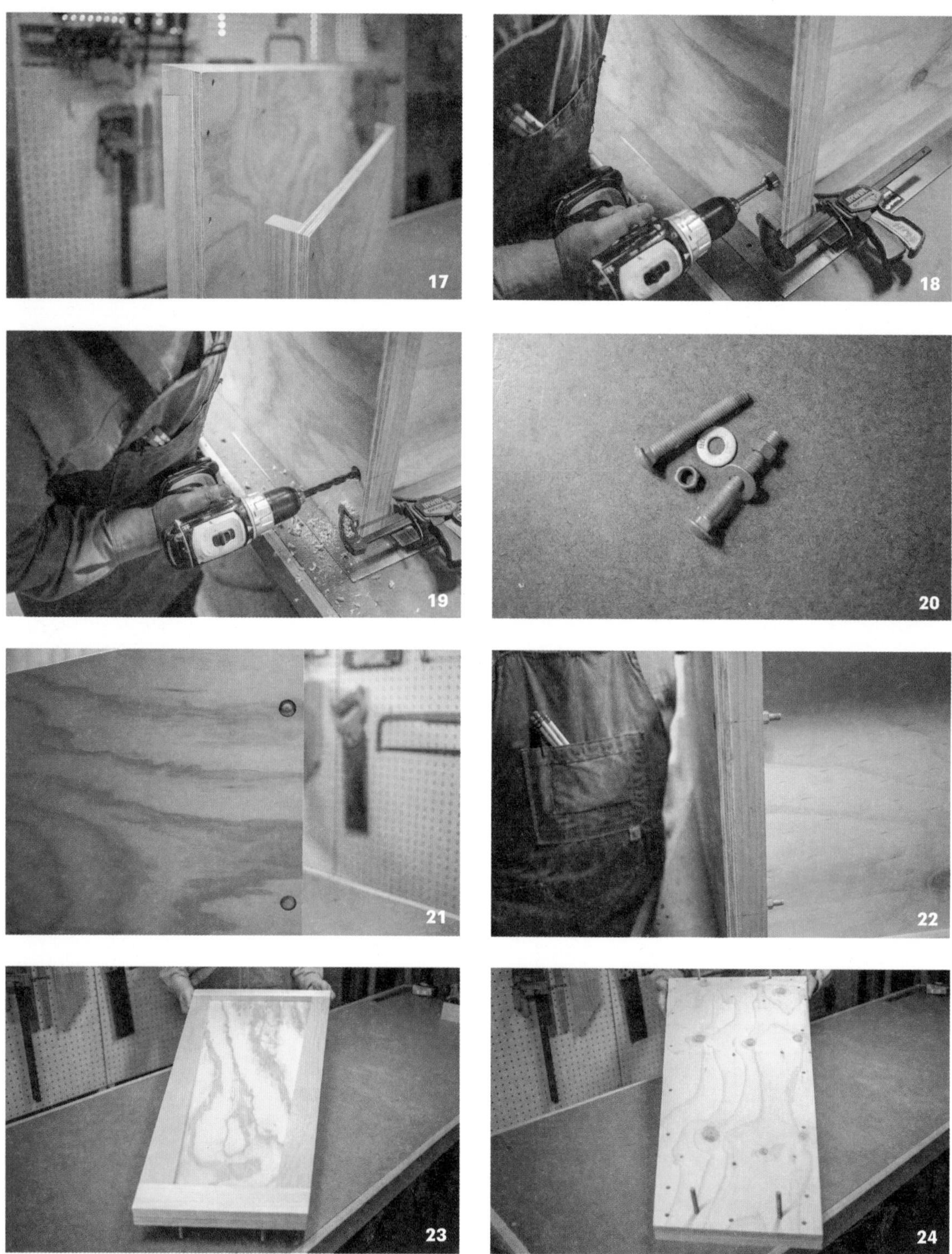
17
18
19
20
21
22
23
24

25

26

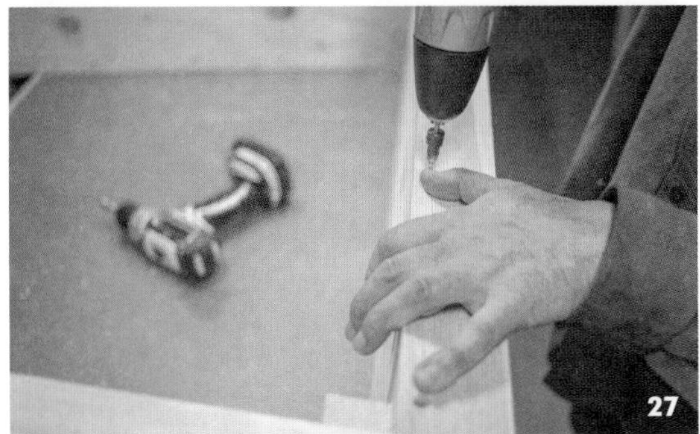

27

28

STEP 7

Installing Trim Molding on the Sides and Front

Install ¾" × 2 ½" pine around the perimeter of both sides. Countersink and screw with 1 ¼" deck screws.

As shown in **figure 25**, attach the ¾" × 2 ½" pine to the two front corners. Countersink and screw with 1 ¼" deck screws.

Once the two corner pieces are attached, install the top and bottom pieces. **(fig. 26)** (See **diagrams C** and **D** on page 162.)

STEP 8

Installing the Bottom

With all four sections bolted together, turn the piece upside down on a level surface.

Attach ¾" × 3 ½" pine around the perimeter of the pieces. Using your thumb and pinky finger as a measuring gauge, countersink and screw with 1 ½" deck screws. **(figs. 27–28)**

STEP 9

Attaching the Lid

Measure and mark the locations of the hinges. Predrill each hole with the ⅛" bit.

HELPFUL HINT: Install one screw to hold the hinge in place, then align the hinge and proceed to install the remaining screws. **(figs. 29–30)**

Install two exterior hinges and screws. **(fig. 31**; see **diagram B** on page 160)

STEP 10

Making the Lid Prop

As shown in **figure 32**, place a piece of punched flat bar in a vise. Using the hacksaw, cut the bar to the proper length.

HELPFUL HINT: Use two pieces of scrap wood to guide the blade of the hacksaw.

Assemble the ¼" × 2" lag screw, ¼" washer, ¼" × ⅜" plastic spacer, and punched flat bar next as shown in **figure 33**.

Predrill a ¼" hole and attach the ¼" lag screw with the wrench, as shown in **figures 34–35**.

With the punched flat bar installed, use a pencil to scribe a mark. **(fig. 36)**

HELPFUL HINT: When drilling large holes, predrill with a smaller bit. This will help guide the larger bit through the wood.

Using the ⅜" bit, drill through the wood. **(fig. 37)**

HELPFUL HINT: To prevent tear-out, use a piece of scrap wood at the exit point of the hole.

Install a ⅜" × 2 ½" carriage bolt, washer, and two nuts. Tighten down the nuts with the wrench.

Align the carriage bolt threads with the holes of the punched flat bar. **(figs. 38–40)**

Repeat the instructions to install the second lid prop.

29
30
31
32
33
34
35
36

37

38

39

40

NOTES

12.

Potting Table

This three-tiered potting table will be the centerpiece of your garden. Keep your favorite tools within reach on the handy pegboard. The lower shelf is a great place to store larger pots and supplies, and the removable panels and two-bucket design make filling containers and flats easier on your back. Once you build this table, you'll wonder why you never used one before.

Materials Needed

HARDWARE:

- **(1)** 1 lb. box of ¼" deck screws
- **(1)** 1 lb. box of 1 ½" deck screws
- **(1)** 1 lb. box of 2 ½" deck screws
- **(4)** #8 × ¾" lath screws
- **(2)** 20" × 15" × 7" black polypropylene bus tubs
- **(2)** sheets of 220-grit sandpaper

TOOLS:

- Pencil
- Try square
- Straight edge
- Tape measure
- Clamps
- Jigsaw or coping saw
- Cordless screw gun or corded drill
- #6 countersink drill bit
- Magnetic tip holder with a #2 Phillips insert bit
- 1 ⅜" Forstner bit
- ⅛" drill bit
- Miter saw or miter box (optional)
- Table saw (optional)

Diagram B
Back

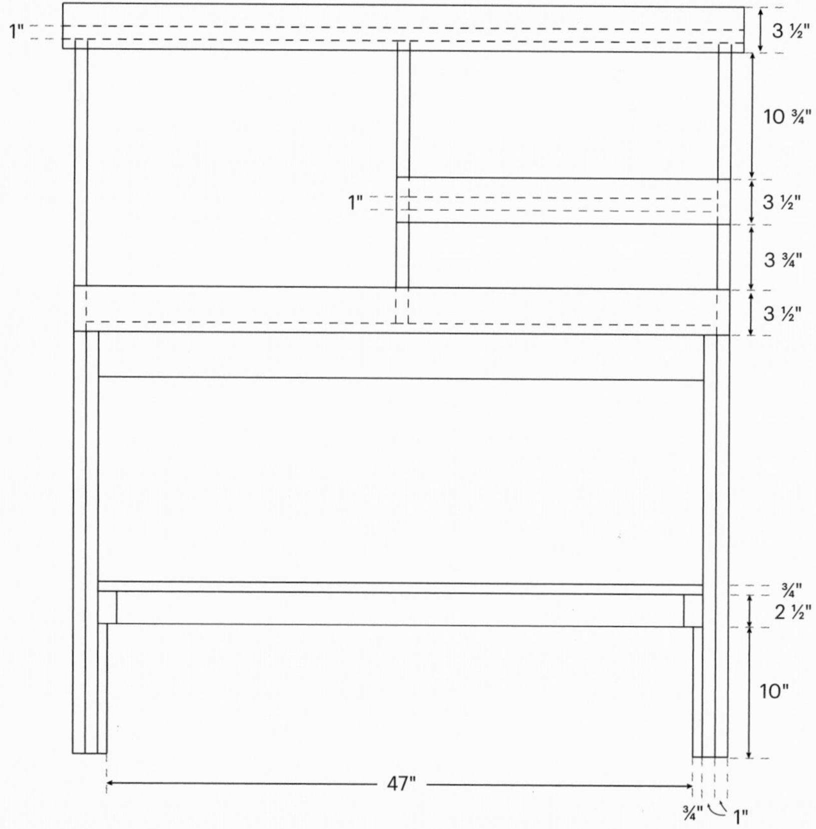

Diagram A

Materials & Cutting

A Deck lids (6): ¾" × 7 ¼" × 16"
B Deck subframe (2): 1 ½" × 3 ½" × 48 ½"
C Deck subframe (2): 1 ½" × 3 ½" × 18"
D Tub rails (2): 1 ½" × 1 ½" × 45 ½"
E Deck border (2): ¾" × 3 ½" × 16"
F Deck border (2): ¾" × 3 ½" × 50 ½"
G Deck border cleats (2): ¾" × 1 ¼" × 45 ½"
H Front legs (4): ¾" × 3 ½" × 32"
I Back legs (2): 1" × 5 ½" × 32"
J Shelf supports (4): ¾" × 3 ½" × 10"
K Shelf frame: 1 ½" × 2 ½" × 48 ½"
L Shelf frame: 1 ½" × 2 ½" × 19"
M Shelf frame: 1 ½" × 2 ½" × 45 ½"
N Shelf frames (2): 1 ½" × 2 ½" × 20 ½"
O Shelf slats (6): ¾" × 3 ½" × 48 ½"
P Shelf unit sides (2): 1" × 5 ½" × 54 ½"
Q Shelf unit vertical support: 1" × 5 ½" × 21 ¾"
R Small shelf: 1" × 5 ½" × 24 ¾"
S Top shelf: 1" × 5 ½" × 54 ½"
T Shelf backer strip: ¾" × 3 ½" × 54 ½"
U Shelf backer strip: ¾" × 3 ½" × 52 ½"
V Shelf backer strip: ¾" × 3 ½" × 26 ½"
Pegboard (not shown): ⅛" × 21 ¾" × 24 ¾"

1" × 8" × 96" — Knotted Pine (1 board)

1" × 5 ½" × 96" — Knotted Pine (4 boards)

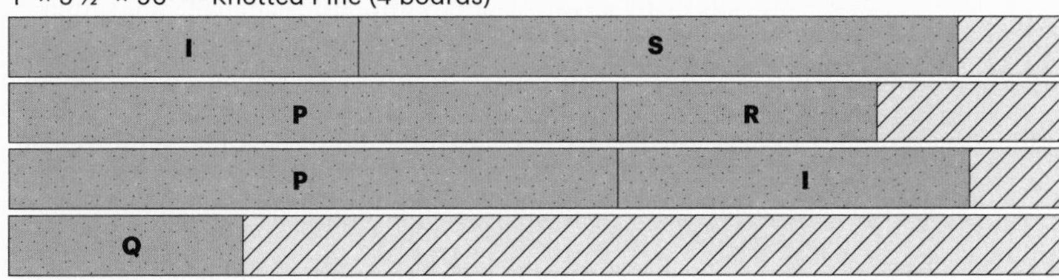

1" × 4" × 96" — Knotted Pine (10 boards)

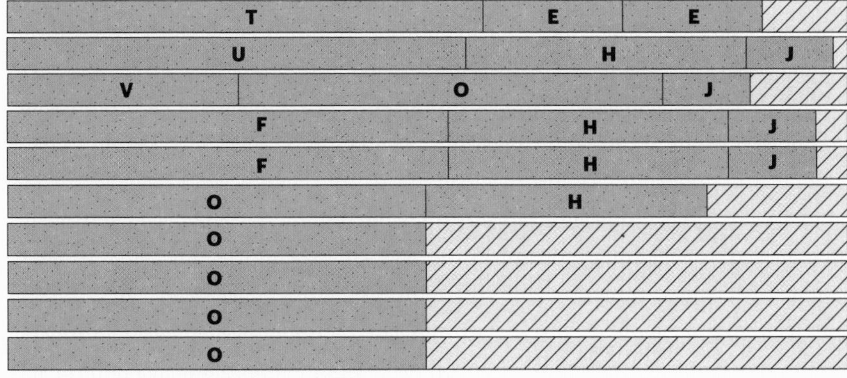

2" × 4" × 96" — Pine (2 boards)

C C B

B

2" × 3" × 96" — Pine (2 boards)

D 1 ½" × 1 ½" × 96" — Pine (1 board)

G ¾" × 1 ¼" × 96" — Knotted Pine (1 board)

Diagram C
Front

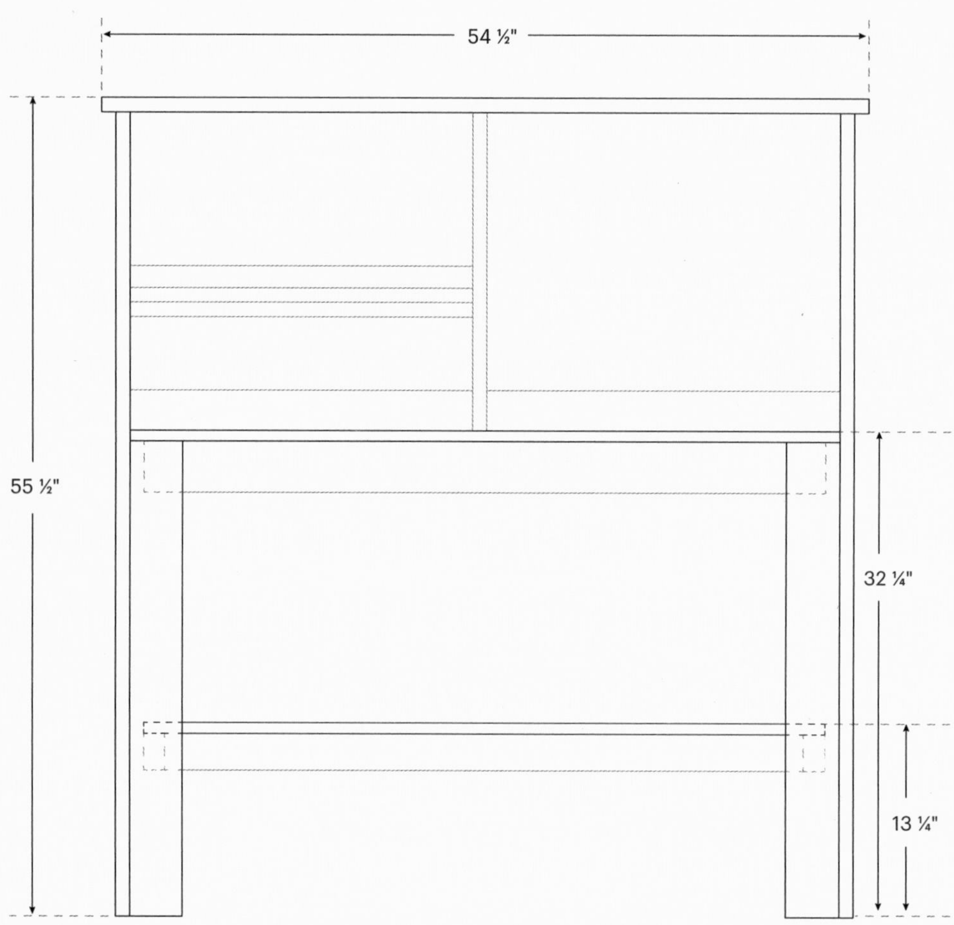

Diagram D
Top

Diagram E
Side

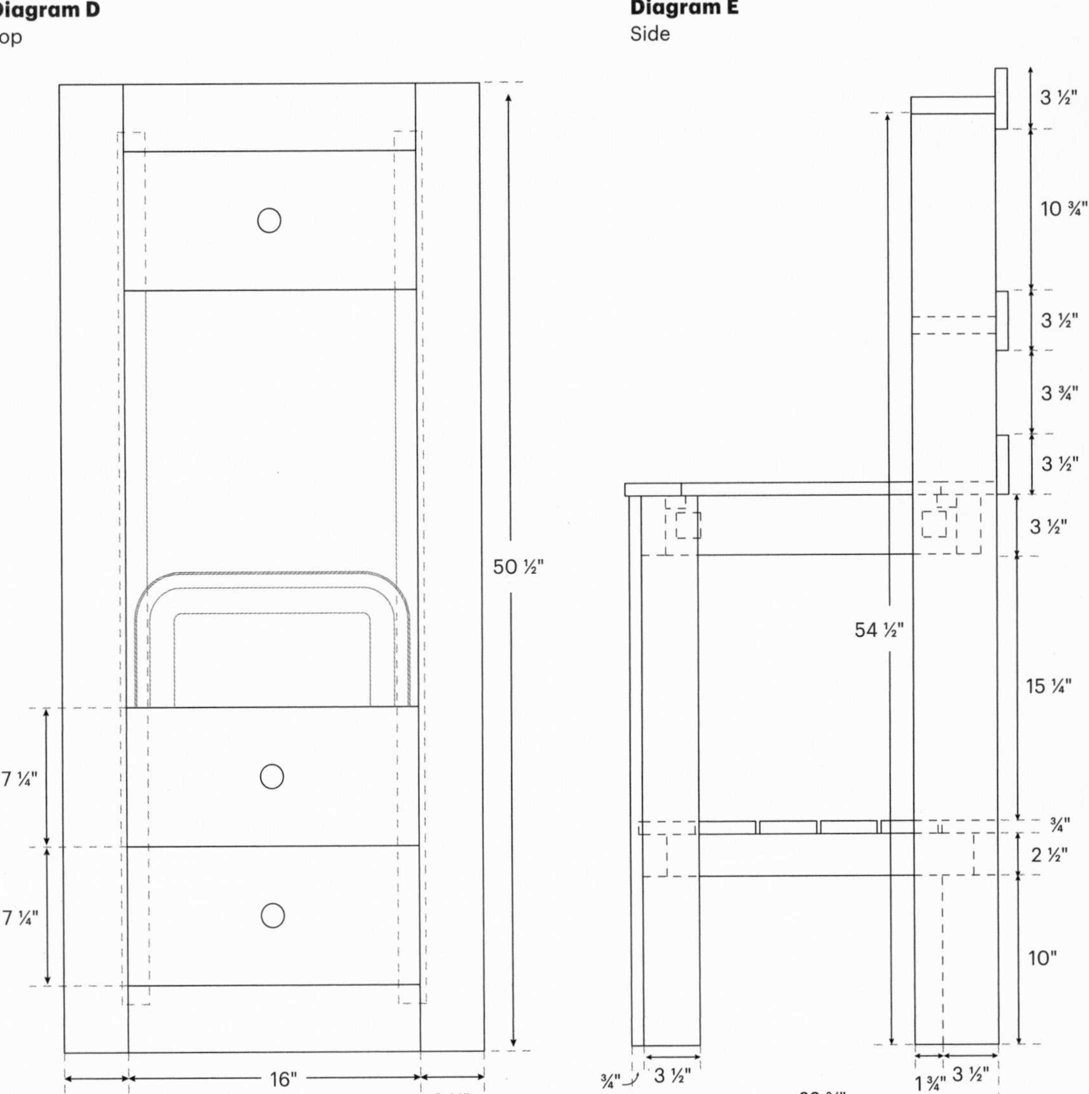

STEP 1

Making the Deck Lids

Select and cut six pieces of pine, each measuring ¾" × 7 ¼" × 16".

HELPFUL HINT: To find the center point of a board, take a straight edge and scribe diagonal lines from each corner. Where the two lines intersect will determine the center point. **(fig. 1)**

Using the 1 ⅜" Forstner bit, drill a hole through each board's center point. **(fig. 2)**

HELPFUL HINT: Always secure your workpiece to your work surface with clamps. Use a backer board to prevent tear-out.

Sand the six pieces with 220-grit sandpaper. Remove any pencil lines and slightly round over any sharp edges.

STEP 2

Making the Deck Subframe

Select and cut four pieces of 2×4, two measuring 1 ½" × 5 ½" × 48 ½" and two measuring 1 ½" × 3 ½" × 18". Lay out the four pieces on a level work surface. **(fig. 3)**

Attach the four pieces by countersinking and screwing with 2 ½" deck screws. **(fig. 4)**

STEP 3

Making the Tub Rail Spacers

Select a plastic tub and measure the lip and tab as shown in **figures 5–6**. On the tubs I used, I chose 1 ¼" as the measurement needed.

Select a piece of pine and cut out four pieces, each measuring ¾" × 1 ¼" × 2 ¼".

STEP 4

Installing the Tub Rails

Select and cut two pieces of pine, each measuring 1 ½" × 1 ½" × 45 ½". As shown in **figure 7**, place a tub inside of the subframe. Align the spacers along the inner perimeter of the subframe. Align the tub rails onto the spacers as shown in **figure 8**. Attach the rail pieces by countersinking and screwing with 2 ½" deck screws. **(fig. 9)**

STEP 5

Installing the Deck Border

Select and cut four pieces of pine, two measuring ¾" × 3 ½" × 50 ½" and two measuring ¾" × 3 ½" × 16". Install cleats to the underside of the two 50 ½" pieces of the border. **(fig. 10)** These cleats will hold the six lids in place.

Align the border pieces on the subframe and attach by countersinking and screwing with 1 ¼" deck screws. **(figs. 11–12)**

Test fit the six lid pieces. Trim and adjust as needed. **(fig. 13)**

STEP 6

Attaching the Legs

Select and cut four pieces of pine, each measuring ¾" × 3 ½" × 32". Attach the front legs to the subframe as shown in **figure 14**. Countersink and screw with 1 ½" deck screws.

Select and cut two pieces of pine, each measuring 1" × 5 ½" × 32". Attach both rear legs by countersinking and screwing with 1 ½" deck screws. **(fig. 15)**

9

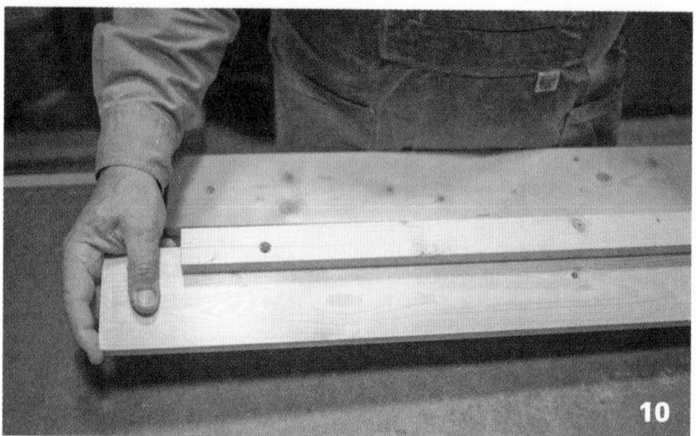
10

11

12

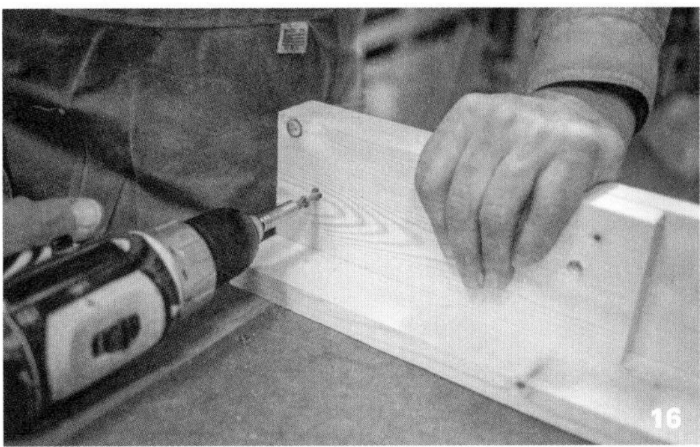

17

STEP 7

Making the Shelf Supports

Select and cut four pieces of pine, each measuring ¾" × 3 ½" × 10". Attach these pieces to the bottom of each leg, creating a resting place for the shelf. Countersink and screw with 1 ¼" deck screws. **(figs. 16–17)**

STEP 8

Building and Installing the Shelf

Select and cut five pieces of 2"× 3" pine, two measuring 1 ½" × 2 ½" × 20 ½", one measuring 1 ½" × 2 ½" × 48 ½", one measuring 1 ½" × 2 ½" × 19", and the last measuring 1 ½" × 2 ½" × 45 ½".

As shown in **figures 18–19**, attach the pieces by countersinking and screwing with 3 ½" deck screws.

Align the shelf frame onto the cleats. Attach the frame to the legs by countersinking and screwing with 2 ½" deck screws. **(figs. 20–21)**

Select and cut six pieces of pine, each measuring ¾" × 3 ½" × 48 ½".

HELPFUL HINT: Create a jig to help you make uniform holes on the shelf slats. **(fig. 22)**

When attaching the shelf slats to the frame, start the first piece at the rear of the shelf. Countersink and screw with 1 ¼" deck screws. As shown in **figure 23**, use ¼" spacers to align the pieces evenly.

As you come to the front shelf piece, use the jigsaw or coping saw to trim the frontpiece around the leg. **(fig. 24)**

18
19
20
21
22
23
24
25

26
27
28
29
30
31
32
33

STEP 9

Making the Shelf Unit

Select and cut two pieces of pine, each measuring 1" × 5 ½" × 54 ½". Attach the pieces by countersinking and screwing with 2 ½" deck screws. **(figs. 25–26)**

Select and cut a piece of pine measuring 1" × 5 ½" × 5 ½".

HELPFUL HINT: Create a jig as shown in **figure 27** to help leave a 1" overhang at the ends of the top shelf.

Attach the top shelf by countersinking and screwing with 3 ½" deck screws. **(fig. 27)**

Select and cut a piece of pine measuring 1" × 5 ½" × 21 ¾". On each end of the board, scribe a mark at 3 ¼". Connect the marks using the straight edge. Starting at one end of the board, measure along the line and mark at 6 ½". Use the try square to draw a line across the mark. Trace around a one-quart paint can to create an arch. **(fig. 28)** Using clamps, secure the piece to your work surface. Use the jigsaw or coping saw to cut along the line. **(fig. 29)**

HELPFUL HINT: When cutting with a jigsaw, cut next to the line and sand the piece up to the line. **(fig. 30)**

Use the try square to align the piece. Attach by countersinking and screwing with 3 ½" and 2 ½" deck screws. **(figs. 31–32)**

Select and cut a piece of pine measuring 1" × 5 ½" × 24 ¾". As shown in **figure 33**, attach the small shelf by countersinking and screwing with 2 ½" deck screws.

Select and cut three pieces of pine, measuring ¾" × 3 ½" × 54 ½", ¾" × 3 ½" × 52 ½", and ¾" × 3 ½" × 26 ½". Attach the shelf backer strips by countersinking and screwing with 1 ½" deck screws. (**fig. 34**; see **diagram E** on page 179.)

Select and cut a piece of pegboard measuring ⅛" × 21 ¾" × 24 ¾". Attach the board with four #8 × ¾" lath screws. **(fig. 35)**

34

35

Resources

REFERENCES

The Wood Database, accessed March 2, 2016, http://www.wood-database.com/.

Lowe's, "Lumber Buying Guide: Common Wood Defects," http://www.lowes.com/projects/build-and-remodel/lumber-buying-guide/project.

The Old Farmer's Almanac, "What The Heck Is A Garden Hod?," accessed March 2, 2016, http://www.almanac.com/blog/made-usa/what-heck-garden-hod.

Barbara Pleasant, "Choose the Best Garden Fence," Mother Earth News, April/May 2010, http://www.motherearthnews.com/organic-gardening/pest-control/best-garden-fence-zmaz10amzraw.aspx.

Derek H. Weiss, "The Cold Frame Handbook," Finger Lake Institute, Hobart and William Smith Colleges, https://www.hws.edu/fli/pdf/cold_frame.pdf.

ONLINE TOOL & SUPPLY STORES

www.GarretWade.com

www.HighlandWoodworking.com

www.LeeValley.com

www.Rockler.com

www.TraditionalWoodworker.com

www.Woodcraft.com

Acknowledgments

Thank you to everyone at Princeton Architectural Press who participated in the publication of this book—especially Tom Cho, Barbara Darko, and Mia Johnson, who took the time to experience my workshops and learn firsthand how I teach my novice woodworkers. A special thank you to Rob Shaeffer for having the wisdom to see into the future and help me get my voice heard. Thanks to Whitney Freeman of Henny Penny Farm in Ridgefield, Connecticut, for letting us photograph many of the projects in her beautiful garden.

Published by
Princeton Architectural Press
A McEvoy Group company
37 East Seventh Street
New York, New York 10003
202 Warren Street
Hudson, New York 12534
Visit our website at www.papress.com

Printed and bound in China by 1010 Printing International
20 19 18 17 4 3 2 1 First edition

Editor: Barbara Darko
Designer: Mia Johnson

Special thanks to: Janet Behning, Nicola Brower, Abby Bussel, Erin Cain, Tom Cho, Benjamin English, Jenny Florence, Jan Cigliano Hartman, Lia Hunt, Valerie Kamen, Simone Kaplan-Senchak, Diane Levinson, Jennifer Lippert, Kristy Maier, Sara McKay, Eliana Miller, Jaime Nelson Noven, Esme Savage, Rob Shaeffer, Sara Stemen, Paul Wagner, and Joseph Weston of Princeton Architectural Press
—Kevin C. Lippert, publisher

Library of Congress Cataloging-in-Publication Data
Names: Perrone, Frank, author.
Title: Build it yourself : weekend projects for the garden / Frank Perrone ; photographs by Nicholas Perrone ; illustrations by Christopher Perrone.
Other titles: Weekend projects for the garden
Description: First edition. | New York, New York : Princeton Architectural Press, [2017]
Identifiers: LCCN 2016032184 | ISBN 9781616893385 (alk. paper)
Subjects: LCSH: Garden structures—Design and construction—Amateurs' manuals. | Garden ornaments and furniture—Design and construction—Amateurs' manuals.
Classification: LCC TH4961 .P48 2017 | DDC 690/.89—dc23
LC record available at https://lccn.loc.gov/2016032184

NOTES